BOOK 1 OF THE BEGINNING'S
END TRILOGY`

# Beginning's End

EMILY PICKARD

*For Mom, who's been there every step of the way.*

Dear Reader,

I'm so excited you're about to take this journey with my main characters Amelia and Kathleen. Enjoy tagging along with these two as they visit some of my favorite places. Ireland is close to my heart—I hope you enjoy this story as much as I enjoyed writing it.

Sláinte!

~Emily

# Table of Contents

1 .................................................................................. 7

2 .................................................................................. 12

3 .................................................................................. 14

4 .................................................................................. 17

5 .................................................................................. 21

6 .................................................................................. 25

7 .................................................................................. 31

8 .................................................................................. 37

9 .................................................................................. 44

10 ................................................................................ 48

11 ................................................................................ 57

12 ................................................................................ 64

13 ................................................................................ 70

14 ................................................................................ 76

15 ................................................................................ 84

16 ................................................................................ 89

17 ................................................................................ 98

18 ................................................................................ 101

19 ................................................................................ 106

20 ................................................................................ 117

21 ................................................................................ 124

22 ................................................................................ 135

23 ................................................................................ 140

24 ................................................................................ 154

25 ................................................................................ 159

26 ................................................................................ 161

27 ................................................................................ 166

28 .................................................................................... 177

29 .................................................................................... 184

30 .................................................................................... 191

Kathleen and Amelia's Mix (by Amelia) ......................................... 194

ACKNOWLEDGEMENTS .......................................................... 195

ABOUT THE AUTHOR ............................................................... 198

# 1

I stood in the hustle bustle of the International Terminal at SFO, waiting next to the bank of Aer Lingus counters with my bag propped against my leg. Another PA Announcement reminded me why: "This is a security reminder. Please maintain control of baggage at all times." Got it. A group walked by and grabbed my attention—those accents. I got another flutter of excitement. Ireland! We were finally going back.

It seemed like a lifetime ago that I'd last stood here, about to visit my best friend Kathleen on her school exchange to Dublin. More innocent and hopeful, a bit more blinded by youth. Definitely less bruised ...

"Amelia!"

I looked up and couldn't keep the smile off my face. I hadn't seen Kathleen in way too long. After living together and then sharing the same block, I was used to seeing her just about every day. We had met during freshman orientation at Chico State and never looked back. Oh, the stories we could tell! About a year ago, I'd made the move from Chico to San Francisco and things just hadn't been the same. Technically I hadn't been the same when I left and was now trying to fix that, starting with this trip. San Francisco was only three hours away but hard for frequent visits, and phone conversations here and there weren't cutting it.

Her reddish-brown hair danced along her shoulders as she rushed towards me, then wrapped me in a big hug. "Hello, friend," I said, in greeting. "Ready for our grand adventure?"

"*Am* I? Bring on the *movies* and the *Bailey's* ... Oh, I'm so excited. I can't believe we're finally going back! What to do first."

We turned and wheeled our bags over to one of the check-in counters. No line. This definitely boded well for our trip. We checked in quickly, surrendering our bags, then made our way to security.

"Did you stash your pistol?"

"Shut up. They'll believe you!"

I could only smile. We made it through the scanner without incident. As we walked to the gate I glanced around, taking it all in and wondering where everyone was going. The cute thirty-something guy in his tailored suit rushing by with his cell phone to his ear ... the sleepy little girl in her pajamas, holding her mom's hand and watching the airplanes out the windows. I just loved that it was us going somewhere exciting, too.

"So are Anne and James already there?" Kathleen asked.

My thoughts turned to our conversation from a few nights ago.

*"They're finally doing it!"*

*"Doing what? Who?"*

*"Anne and James."*

*"Wait ... No ... Weren't they—"*

*"Yup, last night."*

*"No way! Are you serious?"*

*"He asked her. She said yes."*

*"They're getting married?! After all this time ..."*

My sister was really doing it. She was getting married. I still couldn't quite believe it. It all felt so—surreal.

"Yeah, they've been there a week already. They wanted some time to make arrangements. They called and booked the church from here, but wanted to meet and work with the local merchants for flowers and all. I get to make my own bouquet."

"Very nice, Miss Maid-of-Honor. I'm thinking ... black roses!"

"Very funny." My heart *did* ache a bit thinking back on how my own happiness had been so suddenly cut short, but I really was happy for my sister who had waited so long for this day. "I can still be happy for others, especially my twin sister. Now give the nice lady your boarding pass and let's get this show on the road."

Kathleen laughed and acquiesced, but gave me an I'm-bringing-this-back-up-later look. We filed in with the rest of the passengers and made our way down the jet bridge, then boarded the plane. Our seats were halfway back and smack in the middle of the center section. Guess our window and aisle request got lost. Oh well, at least we had the giant TV screen in front of us. It made me think of the closing scene in *Say Anything*.

Kathleen and I shared a look, and she said, "Wait for the ding?" We cracked up and took our seats.

The next few minutes were a flurry of activity as people made their way to their seats and got settled. I saw lots of magazines being pulled out and earphones going in. Not a bad idea. Kathleen tried to get the attention of a flight attendant to ask for a Baileys while I pulled out the in-flight magazine to check on the movies. "Sheesh, can't you even wait until we take off? We're not First Class," I whispered to her. She finally sat back in defeat, and we were on our way.

I awoke with a start and slowly blinked my eyes. The first thing I saw was a watery glass of Bailey's on my tray table. *When did that come down?* The second was Kathleen, staring at me.

"Well g'morning, sunshine!"

"I fell asleep?" I could not get my brain to cooperate.

"Yeah, right after takeoff. I swear you have narcolepsy."

I fall asleep very easily in cars, trains ... planes.

"You missed the first movie!"

"Well thanks for my, uh, breakfast." I eyed the creamy, tannish liquid, then took a sip. Not bad. "I feel like we're back in college."

"Hey, it was just that one time and you said it was okay because it was St. Patrick's Day." We both laughed at the memory of green eggs and Sierra Nevada Pale Ale at 7:00 a.m. "But really, are you okay?"

"I'm *fine*." I was determined not to think about *him*, especially at the start of such an exciting vacation. I'd wasted enough energy after the breakup. Certainly enough tears. "Just putting in long hours to get up to speed at work—proving myself and all that. I'm so excited my time has finally come, and I don't want to blow it."

"Well alright then. If you're sure it's just that."

"I'm sure."

We clinked glasses.

"You *have* worked hard, so congrats again. How long has it been now? What's the name again?"

There was a time I would have talked with Kathleen nightly, giving her blow-by-blows of my days—especially new jobs. We really had drifted.

"Almost two months, and it's West Coast Press. I love it! I really do. And they were so great giving me this time off."

We fell into a companionable silence, Kathleen returning to her magazine and me scanning the crowd. There was the little girl from the terminal, still in her PJs but now clutching a teddy bear. I wished I was in PJs just then. In the row behind her a couple spoke in hushed tones as the man next to them sat with head back against the seat, mouth wide open, sawing logs. The smell of dinner wafted down the aisle. Mmm ... the chicken or the beef? Suddenly Kathleen smacked me.

"Put it on Channel 9, quick!"

I fumbled with my headset and tried to jam the metal piece into the little hole on the armrest, wondering what could be so darn important. Dropkick Murphy's! Kathleen and I loved the Celtic punk band and had seen them in concert a few years back. We grinned at each other and started bouncing in our seats, much to the chagrin of the lady next to me. I grinned at her sheepishly and settled back down.

The flight attendant was just coming to us with her delicious-smelling cart. She informed us there was only chicken left (*what's wrong with it?*), and handed us our trays.

"We should get *two* Bailey's for this," Kathleen muttered to me.

Dinner was actually good, chicken and rice in a nice creamy sauce, and with digestion and the general hum of the plane the sleepies set in. Shades were being pulled; earphones were going back on. I could see Kathleen's eyes drooping also.

"See you in Ireland?" I asked.

"Yeah, we're gonna have a big day tomorrow. Sleep would be good."

We both changed to the Irish Aires station on the radio and snuggled down with our pillows and blankets.

# 2

Kathleen and I stood at the curb waiting for the next available cab. I texted Anne to let her know we'd landed safely and now planned to officially start our adventure. The sleep on the plane had given me good energy, despite the drizzly gray day that greeted us when we stepped outside the airport doors.

"Where to first?" Kathleen asked. "Guinness Brewery? Carrolls? St. Stephen's Green?" We just looked at each other.

"Thing Mote!" we yelled in unison, then laughed. Thing Mote, currently known as O'Donoghue's, was a pub in Dublin that Kathleen and I had frequented when she'd lived and studied at Trinity College. Many pints had been consumed there, many great memories made.

"Remember when you wanted to meet that cute fiddle player—"

"And tripped up the stairs, falling on my knees in front of him?" Kathleen finished. "Yes, I do."

We both laughed again.

"Hey, at least he bought you a pint and danced with you later."

"True," Kathleen said, smiling at the memory.

"How about we check in at the B&B," I suggested. "Decide from there?"

"That sounds good. Where are we staying again?"

I dug around in my purse, searching for the little business card I had received in the mail from Anne. "It's called Baggot Court Townhouse. Doesn't that sound great? Like something from *The Hobbit*."

"Yes, that's how we should choose our accommodations," Kathleen said.

"There's also a free full breakfast."

"Now *that* works."

Finally a cab eased to the curb next to us and a nice-looking, older gentleman jumped out to help us with our bags.

"Let me, girls. Where are we going today?" I admired his plaid golf cap as he bent to put my bag in the trunk.

"We're going to the Baggot Court Townhouse," I said, the business card still clutched in my hand. "In Dublin. I have the address here ..."

"Ah, I know where it is; no problem. Nice place." He put Kathleen's bag in the trunk and slammed it shut. "Hop in, girls."

We slid into the backseat and buckled up.

"Now, where are we from?"

"California," Kathleen and I said at the same time; then she gestured for me to continue.

"We're both from Northern California," I added. "Back for a visit and to see my sister get married."

"Ah, that's grand. Nice occasion. Well, welcome back then. I always say, have as many holidays as you can, because we're only here for a short time."

"I like that," I said, and Kathleen agreed. We then fell into silence as we settled back and gazed out the windows. I drank it all in. The smells, the quaint houses ... I realized I had a goofy grin on my face and turned to see Kathleen staring at me.

"Shut up!"

Kathleen laughed. "Nah, I get it. I'm happy to be back too."

We shared a small squeal, caught an amused glance in the rearview mirror from Michael the driver, and continued drinking in the sights. As Dublin drew closer and the buildings grew taller, I couldn't help but heave a sigh, part excitement and part contentment. We were back.

# 3

The cab rolled to a stop in front of a tall building on Lower Baggot Street. *So that was where the name came from.* We got out and looked up at it. Red brick wall, wrought-iron fencing, windows with white frilly curtains, solid red door. Just as I had pictured.

I handed Kathleen some money for the cab fare.

"I'll head inside and check us in," I said, as she helped Michael heave our bags out of the car. Walking up the steps, I couldn't help doing a little jig and hoped I didn't look *too* much like a tourist. I reached out to grip and turn the knob, but nothing happened. I put a little more pressure on the door, finally pushing my shoulder into it; still nothing. Taking a step away, I glanced around to make sure I'd had no witnesses. When I looked back at the door, I saw the sign: Guests—Use key / Visitors— Please ring bell. *Ah.* I rang the bell, heard a buzz and click, and tried the knob again. This time it pushed right open.

"Having a bit of trouble with the door? Sorry, I would have buzzed you sooner but wasn't close to the desk." A very attractive man was making his way towards me up a narrow hallway, trying to hide a smile. He was a bit taller than me, which is not hard since I'm 5'3". "Welcome to Baggot Court Townhouse. I am Patrick. How can I help you?" I glanced at his name tag—Padraig.

"My friend and I have a reservation for tonight. It should be under Amelia. Is it too early to check in?"

We heard a thump at the front door. Padraig turned and opened it. "This must be Amelia's friend. Welcome to Baggot Court," he said with a twinkle in his eye. Kathleen just looked at us. "Yes, I did see your name. Your room should be ready. Just let me check which number."

He walked back down the hallway to what appeared to be a workstation, and we followed. I took a moment to study him as he bent his head to a computer screen. Brown, thick, curly hair gave him a boyish look but the lines in his face made me guess mid-thirties. I was admiring the muscles in his hands, as he typed with sure strokes, when he looked up and caught my gaze. He grinned and looked back down. I looked away, feeling a flush, only to find Kathleen studying me. I widened my eyes in a silent *"What?"* and turned away to study the rest of the small lobby area. Dark wood counter and lower wall paneling, light cream walls to give a sense of space, a small padded bench under a wall rack filled with pamphlets of restaurants and tours. There was even a door propped open, looking to lead to a small patio area. We'd have to check that out later. I turned back to see Padraig handing Kathleen a set of keys.

"There you go, ladies. Best room in the house. Top floor, just at the head of the stairs. Sorry, there's no lift."

"Oh, that's alright," I said. "We're used to it—we can manage."

He looked at me a little quizzically and then led the way back along the small hallway. "Just this way," he said, as he gestured up a long stairway opposite the front doors. We thanked him and started to climb, pulling and bumping our way up six flights of stairs. Thank goodness for rolling luggage! By the time we got to the top all I could do was open the door, drop my bag on the ground, and flop onto a bed. Kathleen followed suit, and we lay in silence for a few moments, catching our breath. Finally I heard stirring from the other side of the room.

"So what's the plan again? How long do we get to play in Dublin before we have to head out?"

"Well, the wedding is in ten days, and I told Anne we'd be there four days ahead," I answered. "Doolin is on the opposite coast from here, so depending on where we want to go and what we want to see, it could take a few hours or a few days; so however we want to spread out the time. I'd like to just drive and see where we want to stop along the way."

"I vote we stay in Dublin for a couple of days so you can get to know Padraig better." I threw a pillow at her. "Oh, there are a few places I'd like to revisit too—like my old dorm. Then we can tour the countryside."

"My thoughts too. I love touring the brewery and just hanging around city centre. Sounds great. So what do you say we go grab a pint before we're out cold for the night?"

"Good idea," she laughed, stifling a yawn. "Temple Bar?"

"You read my mind."

We took turns freshening up a bit, then grabbed sweaters (you never knew where the day could take you) and made our way back downstairs. Padraig was still at the reception area and looked up from the magazine he'd been reading.

"Everything alright, ladies?" he called.

"Oh yes," I replied. "We're just going out for a bit. Grab a pint, maybe some food."

"Need any recommendations? I know all the good spots."

"Oh, no thanks," I answered. "Some of our favorites are in Temple Bar, so we're heading that way."

"Ah, so you *have* visited here before."

"Yes, a few times. And Kathleen lived here for a bit." I looked over and she nodded with a smile.

"Well, that's grand. Have a lovely evening. Don't forget your keys—the second one opens the front door."

We thanked him and pushed open the interior glass door, then the big red front door. Stepping onto the front landing, we were immersed in city life once more.

# 4

The area of pubs and shops known as Temple Bar was about a fifteen-minute walk from the B&B, so we set out on foot for a nice stroll. The sun was high in the sky, and the air was refreshingly brisk. Quite a nice early-fall day. Suddenly Kathleen threw her arms around me and gave a tight squeeze. I jumped, then hugged her back.

"Oh, isn't it gorgeous! We really are back. Finally!"

I smiled back at her. "Oh, hey. We mentioned Thing Mote earlier. Want to stop in on our way? If you're—strong enough."

"Very funny," she replied, but laughed. "For sure! It seems only appropriate."

We continued walking and passed small, brightly colored storefronts of florists, newsstands, neighborhood pubs. Lots of folks bustled about, greeting each other and doing last-minute errands before heading home for the evening. We wandered along, taking it all in but trying not to be too nosy. People smiled as we walked by. I just couldn't get over how great it was to be in Dublin again. It was four years or so since Kathleen lived here, longer for Anne, yet everything felt so familiar and comfortable.

"Hey! Look where we are."

I came to and looked around. More cars were zooming by and a bus drove past rather close—city centre! Just across the street, tall, wrought-iron gates stood at attention. Kathleen grabbed my hand and pulled me toward them.

"Let's walk through St. Stephen's Green on the way to Grafton."

Grafton St. is a main thoroughfare through Dublin's city centre, connecting the many pubs and shops in the area.

"Yes, let's," I replied, laughing as I got caught up in her excitement.

We walked through the giant gates and took a deep breath. St. Stephen's Green was such a respite from the bustling city only a few feet away. The beautiful greenery and towering trees, cleaner-feeling air, diminished sound. We strolled along one of the many pathways and tried not to grin too much. An older couple walked towards us arm in arm, bundled up in wooly jackets and hats. The woman smiled at us and the gentleman touched the tip of his hat with a "Girls." We smiled back.

I took a deep breath and felt my blood pressure go down. I had not thought starting the new job was too stressful and was so happy to have it, but strolling next to Kathleen through this park was so peaceful and a much-needed slowdown. We made our way along the path to one of the exit gates on the other side. The taxis and buses were back, and we darted across the street to officially enter the shopping area. Grafton!

We walked down the wide brick street and exclaimed as we saw our favorite shops—Butlers chocolate shop, Bewley's cafe, Carrolls souvenir shop. A few buskers were playing lively tunes on fiddles and tin whistles and drawing crowds. Little carts stood here and there, loaded with jewelry and trinkets. I could have stayed there all day and browsed each and every one, but I forced myself to keep strolling. We had lots more country to see. When we finally came to the corner of Suffolk and glanced down the street, seeing the oh-so-familiar pub front, we exchanged glances and quickened our pace.

Kathleen pulled open the door and ushered me in. We stood just inside, taking it all in. Polished wood counter along the left wall, raised stage area with plush seats on the opposite wall, stairs to our right leading to a loft. The bartender noticed us, so we stepped up to the bar. He greeted us with a smile.

"Welcome, ladies. This your first time here?"

"No," I replied, "but it's been a while. I remember this as Thing

Mote, so I was seeing what had changed."

"Ah yes." He seemed impressed. "That's a ways back."

"My sister lived here a few years ago. My friend as well," I said, indicating Kathleen.

"Very good," he said and smiled at her. "What can I get you then?"

"Jameson and ginger, please," Kathleen said, ordering the drink she'd discovered while living here.

"Nice call," I said. "Start with a kick." The bartender placed the glass in front of her and turned to me.

"Bulmers, please." I'd been waiting for this! Cider was just not the same in the US. I pulled out a twenty-euro note and put it on the bar. "First one's on me," I said, as I grabbed my drink.

"Name's Tom if you need anything else," he said, with a nod.

We thanked him and turned to find a seat. "Shall we sit up on the stage?" I asked, feeling mischievous.

"*Yes,* I think we should," Kathleen replied and marched up the steps. Her toe caught at the top and she jostled her drink. She stabilized and turned to me with wide eyes.

I was gone. "No way," I managed to get out. Tom cast a curious glance our way, then shook his head and continued cleaning glasses. "Alright, now *that* was awesome."

By this time Kathleen had plopped down into a cushy armchair. "Here's to me!" she yelled and took a swig from her glass.

I laughed, raised my glass to her, and took a sip. Ah, sweet nectar. This was my favorite drink, and Anne's too; so I thought of her and smiled. We had very different personalities but really did enjoy a lot of the same things. The first time we'd discovered Bulmers had been *quite* the night.

"I wonder what Anne and James are doing right now," I said as I took a seat next to Kathleen.

"Probably horribly romantic things."

"I'm sure you're right. Last I talked to her she sounded *deliriously* happy."

"Well good, she deserves it. They both do." Kathleen paused and studied me. "How about you? Maybe not deliriously, but you're happy, right?"

Here we go. I took a deep breath and smiled at her. "Yes, I'm happy."

"You don't have to be, y'know. You went through hell, and not all that long ago." She paused, then continued. "It just feels like you're so far away, and I don't know what's going on in your head."

"Kathleen, I'm *fine* ... really. Sure I have my moments, but work has been a really great outlet. And I know I can always call you. I know it's weird ... I miss you too." I reached out and grabbed her hand, giving it a squeeze.

"And you know what's in my head. I still tell you everything! Truthfully, it's been nice to be distracted and not think about it so much. Maybe I'm avoiding things a bit, but that's all I can do right now. Maybe I'll want to dig back into it, and you'll be the *first* one I call."

"Well, okay then. You know where to find me."

"Now before we get too maudlin ... what's that saying? As you slide down the banister of life, may the splinters never point the wrong direction?" We laughed, and I held up my glass.

"To that," Kathleen said, as she toasted me.

I raised my glass again and Kathleen did the same. "To Ireland! Sláinte!"

"Sláinte!" she chimed in.

We finished our drinks and stood to take our glasses to the bar. "Ready to head out?" Kathleen nodded, and we waved to Tom as we made our way to the door.

"Take care, ladies. See you again."

"I think he fancied you," I whispered to Kathleen as we started up the sidewalk towards Temple Bar.

"Oh c'mon! You think so?" She pondered this for a moment. "He *was* pretty cute. Maybe we'll just have to stop in on the way back."

# 5

Temple Bar was a mass of bodies and sound. People gathered on the cobblestone streets, watching street performers or just chatting together in groups. We were standing next to one of our favorite eateries, the Bad Ass Café. We were also standing next to a huge line going in the door and trying to come up with Plan B.

"We could go to the Quays. It shouldn't be too crowded yet, especially upstairs."

"But I was so in the mood for pizza." Kathleen looked a little put out as she scanned the crowd. "Okay, you're right. This could take a while. I guess shepherd's pie is a close second."

"The Quays it is."

We continued up the cobblestone road, working our way through the groups of people until we landed at the Quays. I glanced into the pub area to the left and then wandered up the stairs in front of me. A middle-aged gentleman was smiling down at us from the top landing.

"Table for two, ladies?"

"Yes, please." I reached the top, stood next to him, and smiled. Kathleen joined us, and we all walked to a table against the side wall of the narrow main room. The host handed us our menus and bustled away to cue our server.

"When did it get so formal, I wonder," Kathleen said, as she glanced through the food options.

"Seriously. As long as the interior didn't change. It's still so beautiful. I love all this dark wood."

"Yeah, the feeling definitely hasn't changed. Nice to be cozy and tucked in up here."

The server arrived, and I ordered a Bulmers, perhaps with a little too much excitement. Kathleen glanced at me, then ordered the same.

"Careful you don't over-do it too quick," Kathleen cautioned when he left. "Don't want to get sick of it before the reception." She knew the Bulmers would be free-flowing.

"As if! Bite your tongue. Anne and I always load up when we're over here, and it hasn't happened yet," I replied. "And who are we kidding—shepherd's pie all around!"

We closed our menus and ordered when our server came back with the drinks. "Original, we know," I said, glancing at our matching Bulmers glasses with a chuckle.

"Hey, my favorite meal, ladies. Good choice." He smiled and walked away.

I leaned back and glanced around the room. It was still early in the afternoon and fairly quiet. Only a few tables were taken. I'd been here when it was wall-to-wall people. Some nights there was even a band playing in the corner we were now sitting near. Kathleen and I caught glances, and I could tell she was remembering too.

"We've had some great nights here," she mused. "Remember how crowded it could get—the energy?"

"I do remember some spilled drinks, yes," I answered, with a laugh.

"And that band ... what was their name? Celtic Reign? I wonder if they still play around here."

"Those were the nights," I agreed. "I'm sure it hasn't changed that much. Give it a few hours—this place'll be hopping."

Our food arrived, and the smell made my mouth water. I hadn't realized how hungry I was. Kathleen looked like she wasn't going to wait for hers to cool either. We both took big forkfuls and watched the steam rise, then blew on them a bit and toasted each other. The first mouthful was delicious. No matter how many times I tried to make it at home, it just wasn't the same.

After a few minutes of silence (and scarfing), we looked at each other and grinned.

"I think we were a little hungry," I said as Kathleen took a sip of cider to cool her mouth off.

"No kidding."

I continued to eat in thoughtful silence. I hadn't been in Kathleen's space for so long. It still felt natural, but I had missed it more than I realized. Maybe I *had* been hiding out a bit and needed to make some adjustments. I felt myself frowning and softened my face, then took a deep breath and sat back to find Kathleen looking at me.

"Everything okay?"

"Yeah, sorry ... just thinking."

She studied me for a moment but didn't press the issue. Suddenly a whistling sound pierced the air and I jumped, clenching my fork and bumping my knee on the table.

"Settle down, psycho," Kathleen said when she'd stopped laughing. "Hey, that must be a band warming up. Shall we close out here and head downstairs? I've been waiting to hear some live music."

"Sure," I replied, rubbing my knee. "Sounds great. More Bulmers!"

We paid our bill quickly, anxious to be closer to the music. Now the sound of a banjo floated up to us—much more gentle than the tin whistle. Once outside, we turned right to enter in the next doorway. The room was starting to fill up, but there were still a few open tables and seats at the bar. Kathleen tilted her head towards the bar, I nodded my agreement, and she led us to two open stools in the middle of the long, dark wood counter. The bartender saw us and came over.

"What can I get ya?"

"A Bulmers for her, please," Kathleen answered, "and a Guinness for me."

He slid the cider to Kathleen, and she passed it on to me. "Here's your beloved Bulmers."

"Thank you very much!" I took a long drink and sighed in contentment. "I could never get sick of this stuff, and I'm telling Anne you said that."

"Well, hello again, ladies."

# 6

I started at the voice close to my ear and turned to find Padraig smiling at me. My heart raced, and I hoped it didn't show. I could feel my face heating up too. Great.

"Amelia … Kathleen …." He nodded to us in turn. "Fancy meeting you here."

I seemed to have lost my tongue, so Kathleen jumped in. "We stopped for some early dinner upstairs, heard the band tuning up and came down here to watch."

"Well, these boys are the best. Listen, I have a table at the front with some friends. You're welcome to join." He looked at us questioningly. "The view's much better than back here."

I finally regained myself and exchanged a nod with Kathleen. "That'd be great, thanks."

We laid our money on the bar, grabbed our drinks and turned to follow Padraig. He led us to the front of the room, just to the right of the low dais where the band was setting up. A long wooden table was tucked into the corner with a group of people looking to be our age around it.

"Guys," Padraig began by way of introduction, "this is Amelia and Kathleen, two of my guests at Baggot Court. I thought they could join our rag tag group."

"Oh stop," a dark-haired girl sitting toward the end of the table said. "That'd be brilliant. My friend Sinead couldn't make it, so you'll sit with me. This will be the girl's end of the table."

"This is Cora," Padraig continued, "and these guys here are Liam, Seamus, and David."

The sandy-haired one named Liam leaned forward and said, "You brought these lovely ladies, but not our drinks, mate."

"Ah, you're right. Sorry. Be right back."

Padraig headed back to the bar, and Kathleen and I settled in next to Cora. My eyes followed Padraig for a moment, and next to me Kathleen was repeating her name to Cora. I tuned back in and turned to join their conversation.

"We just arrived from California," Kathleen was saying.

"As in this morning?" Cora was incredulous. "You need to be dancing then. You girls will be asleep in your drinks!"

I found myself being shoved off the bench and onto the dance floor. Kathleen was laughing and clapping her hands as the band started playing. I couldn't stop the grin spreading across my face watching her, and then Cora grabbed my hands and spun me in a circle.

"This is the *most* fun!" I yelled to Kathleen, who just shook her head with a laugh and kept clapping.

The song ended just as Padraig came back with the drinks and Cora left the floor to claim what looked to be a Guinness. Breathless, we were all too happy to follow after her. She turned as we sat down.

"Ever had Guinness with black currant in it? It can help the taste if you're new to it."

"Actually," I said, as Kathleen side-eyed me, "I have. I've also had an incident with Guinness and vodka." Now I had the attention of the table, so I explained the mix-up with black currant juice and currant-flavored vodka. "Pretty good, but talk about a kick!" I laughed.

"That's a bit hardcore," the dark-haired guy named David said, holding my gaze a moment. "I like this one!"

We all laughed, and Padraig clapped him on the back. "My roommate—the party animal."

Suddenly the third guy, Seamus, pushed his knit hat onto his blonde, curly hair and stood as if to leave. "Sorry, folks. The music calls!"

Cora leaned in as he made his way to the dais. "He knows the guys in that band. Sometimes they let him play. We'll see how long he lasts."

Liam laughed and added, "Once he gets into his pints ... Well, last week he fell off the stage." They all laughed at the memory. I turned and watched as Seamus picked up a bodhrán, an Irish drum, and took a seat at the outside of the group. How cool to be able to just join in as the mood struck.

"So what brings you both to Ireland?" Padraig turned back to us, waiting to hear the answer to Cora's question. I realized we hadn't gone that deep into conversation with him at the hotel.

"Amelia's sister is getting married in Doolin," Kathleen replied. "We couldn't miss the chance to be a part of it and come back to visit."

"And Anne would never forgive us," I chimed in.

Padraig nodded in appreciation. "Doolin ... lovely town."

"You could have flown into Shannon," Liam said. "Saved yourself some driving."

"Oh, I know," I answered. "Kathleen and I have wanted to do this for a while now—a friend road trip through Ireland. It was just the perfect opportunity to spend time together and see some of our favorite places again."

"Well, I think it sounds grand," said Cora, with a smile. "Where are you headed?"

Kathleen pointed to the table as if drawing on an invisible map. "We'll head south through the Wicklows towards Killarney, then make our way back up through Tralee and across the Shannon. Stopping along the way as we see fit."

"Maybe kiss the Blarney Stone?" Liam asked, with a grin.

"Perhaps," I laughed. "I've kissed it once. Maybe I could use a refresher."

"Well I haven't," Kathleen said. "So yes, we must. I want to see the castle and grounds too. I've heard they're beautiful."

"Definitely worth a look," agreed Cora.

I took a sip of my cider and glanced around the room. The place was starting to fill up and more people were dancing. Seamus was still playing. I couldn't keep my gaze from returning to Padraig every so often. There was just something so engaging about him. The way his hand looked so strong gripping his pint glass or how cute his hair looked as it curled just over his ear. Even the way he threw his head back to laugh at something Liam said was unabashed and sexy. *Get a grip, girl!* Padraig turned just then to say something to Kathleen, catching my eye. I slid my glance away in what I hoped was a subtle fashion. That *needed* to stop happening.

A rousing song started, and I felt myself being shoved off the bench again. "C'mon, girls!" Cora shouted, and we made our way into the crowd. The singer strummed his guitar as he sang "Whiskey, You're the Devil," and Seamus continued beating his bodhrán. The energy of the crowd was at a peak, and there was laughter and singing all around the room. Hand clapping, foot stomping, people whirling—it was hard not to get pulled in.

I looked over my shoulder to the table. Padraig and David had their heads together and were laughing about something. "He doesn't dance." Cora's voice startled me, making me whip my head to look at her.

"What? Who?" I tried to play it cool.

She gave me a knowing grin. "Padraig's not much of a dancer. Never has been, even when I tried to get him to, at a dance in our seventh year." She chuckled at the memory.

"Oh no, I was just looking around. Lots of men to dance with in here." I smiled to cover my embarrassment.

Cora nodded her approval, hands still clapping, and turned to some people she seemed to know. I noticed Kathleen chatting with

Seamus (*curious!*) and took the opportunity to sit back down at our table. Padraig and David looked up as I took my seat. Liam had wandered off to talk to a girl at the next table.

"Hello again," said Padraig. A smile lit his blue eyes, making them even more captivating. "Enough dancing for a while?"

"Yes." I returned the smile–and took a sip of my cider. "I think Kathleen is going to wear my feet out on this trip."

"So what's on deck for tomorrow? You and Kathleen will spend time in Dublin before setting out on your adventures?"

I nodded. "You'll think it's cheesy, but we want to go to the Guinness Brewery. I love the tour and the view from the Gravity Bar. Kathleen also wants to visit Trinity College. Maybe we can see her old dorm room."

"Brilliant," said David. "Hey, I go to the brewery every so often, it's alright. It created quite an economy for us."

I decided I liked him. He didn't make me blush like Padraig did, but he had a warmth and spirit to him. If he'd lived back in the Bay, we'd be good friends. I noticed Padraig watching me.

"What about you?" I asked, feeling a bit brave and playful. "Do you frequent the brewery even though it's a tourist attraction?"

"Hey, tourism is a big industry. I work in a hotel, right?" Padraig's inflection lilted down at the end and I smiled, loving the distinction. "But yes, to answer your question. I do make the occasional visit. Great view," he finished, with a wink.

I swear my heart skipped a beat. I'd just met this guy! Get a grip, Amelia. Kathleen and Cora returned to the table, giving me something else to focus on. We got into a rousing conversation on the finer points of Dublin and a few more songs played, but Kathleen's eyes kept getting heavy, and I could feel the jet lag pulling on me too.

"Okay everyone," I said. "It's time for us to call it a night, but thank you so much for letting us join you."

"Yes, it was so nice meeting all of you," Kathleen added.

Everyone nodded in agreement and bid us good night; Padraig stood as if to walk us to the front.

"Oh, that's okay," I protested. *Such a gentleman!* "We'll be fine—you don't have to fight your way through this crowd."

"Well, alright then." He tipped his head to us. "It's obviously my night off, but there's a night manager who can help you should you need it."

Right! This brought me back to the fact that we'd spent the evening with our hotel manager, whom we'd just met—random. We thanked him and said good night again to the rest of the table.

We walked to the bar, finishing our pints along the way—and not spilling a drop despite the jostling. Outside, Kathleen looked at me with a grin. "Yeah, that just happened." I giggled. We linked arms and made our way back to the B&B.

# 7

"Good Moooorning, Dublin!"

I almost swallowed my toothbrush as Kathleen shouted into the bathroom. It was seven, and my brain was still a little fuzzy.

"I didn't hear you get up."

"Well, that was the idea." Kathleen was much too perky and delighted with herself. "I'm hungry, so how about we go to breakfast now and I'll shower after?"

"Works for me." I put my damp hair into a bun and grabbed my sweater. Kathleen was already at the door, so I crossed the room and followed her into the hallway. We walked down the stairs and past the reception desk to the breakfast room. I couldn't help glancing around for Padraig, but saw no sign of him. I tried to tell myself I wasn't disappointed.

The breakfast room was small, but high ceilings and light coloring gave it a spacious feel. There looked to be one table per room, and the room was about half full. The hum of hushed voices and lightly clinking tableware was cozy and inviting, and Kathleen and I tucked into a corner table.

A young woman came to take our orders. We were all too happy to ask for the full Irish breakfast (without the black pudding). I moved between tables to get to the sideboard for yogurt and granola as Kathleen grabbed coffee and tea for us. We knew how to effectively load ourselves up for the day.

Our breakfasts arrived soon after, and I eyed my plate hungrily. Eggs, baked beans, steaming tomatoes, a slice of meat, potatoes—mmm!

We dug in, and it was a good ten minutes before we came up to exhale. I finally sat back and took a sip of tea.

"Can we do the Hop On Hop Off bus to get around today? I know it's a little pricey, but I love sitting on the top out in the open and hearing all the history."

"Yeah, sure," Kathleen replied, also sitting back from her plate. "It's supposed to be a beautiful day so might as well take advantage. Can we go to Trinity first and spend the afternoon at the brewery?"

I nodded and took another forkful of food. The early morning crowd was starting to filter out and families with young children were filling up the tables around us. The noise level was slowly rising.

"Do you think any of your former classmates or professors will still be there?" I asked Kathleen.

"I'm not sure. Most likely professors, but I figured on just walking around and seeing what I do."

I went back to my food, trying to finish up. A particularly shrill cry pierced the air. Kathleen looked at me and we seemed to have the same idea. Excusing our way among the tables, we finally made it to the exit door.

I patted my stomach appreciatively as we walked out. "And to think we get that tomorrow, too." Kathleen laughed and agreed as we turned towards the reception area. I glanced towards the desk and there was Padraig, studying something on his computer screen. I felt a little blush coming on. He looked up and smiled.

"Good morning, ladies. Just come from breakfast?" We nodded and expressed our enjoyment. "Glad to hear it. I could use some myself. I should have left when you did." He chuckled. "Not too bad though, just a little slow this morning."

"Thanks again for letting us join you and your friends," I said. "That was such a fun first night."

"Oh, I'm glad you enjoyed it. They all loved meeting you as well.

You were quite the dancer," he said, grinning at Kathleen. "Kept our Cora good company."

"I just couldn't help myself," Kathleen replied. "I love the music!"

"So you two getting ready to head out?"

"Almost," I replied. "We just need to finish getting ready now that we have food in us."

"Well don't let me keep you. I'll see you on your way out."

I turned to follow Kathleen up the hallway to the lobby. As she started up the staircase, she glanced at me over her shoulder.

"We can stay here today if you want. Become thoroughly acquainted with this place. Maybe do a study of the brochures at reception ..."

"Oh c'mon. We're on vacation—thousands of miles from home. What a bad time to develop a crush."

"Hmm. Bad. Yes ..." She grinned.

We stood at a tall, wrought-iron fence next to Trinity College. I had forgotten how large and austere it was. The iron gates and stone walls of the buildings just beyond were menacing and beautiful at the same time. Next to me, Kathleen was quiet and taking it in as well. I wondered what she was thinking.

"It's been a while," I said. "Do you think things will look the same to you?"

Kathleen looked at me, and there seemed to be some apprehension in her eyes. Maybe that was what she'd been thinking.

"Only one way to find out," she said.

Walking onto the grounds was like walking back in time. The buildings dated to the late 1700s and seemed to carry a certain magic with them, as if they could tell countless secrets. I loved that they remained largely unchanged.

A few groups of people milled about, taking in the campus and reading the history on the different buildings. I'm sure some students were mixed in, heading off to a class or meeting. Next to me, Kathleen was quietly glancing around. A low ringing caught my attention, and I realized it was coming from my pocket. I blushed, feeling as if I shouldn't have such technology in this beautiful, historic place. No one seemed to notice though, so I reached to answer it.

"It's Anne. Why don't I grab it and you go on ahead. I'll be on this bench."

Kathleen nodded, and I swear I saw a little relief in her eyes. Maybe this was more emotional for her than I'd realized.

"Hey!" It was so good to hear Anne's voice, especially over here. So many good memories.

"Hello, sister! I finally hear your voice."

"I know. What are you guys doing right now?"

"We're at Trinity so Kathleen can visit her old stomping grounds, but enough about us. How are *you* guys? How's wedding stuff coming along?"

"Oh, you know … no matter how much you plan, things never go as smoothly as you want. The wedding venue is a little farther from the hotel than we thought, so we're trying to figure out transportation for everyone. And the bridal party dresses just arrived and one looks longer than the others—"

"Oh right, our dresses! You still haven't told me which color you finally chose. The orange just to screw with Kathleen?" I pictured orange with Kathleen's reddish hair and laughed. Anne must have thought the same thing, because she joined in.

"No, you both will be pleasantly surprised. I wouldn't do that to you guys. Besides, that color would ruin my wedding pictures."

We both cracked up. Oh, it was nice to hear my sister's voice. We really were best friends (beside Kathleen, of course) and were always there for each other, even when we disagreed. It was hard hearing her even a bit stressed.

"Well, I hope things work out. Is Mom there yet—to shorten the dress with her mad seamstress skills? And are there cabs we can order to drive people to the wedding?"

"Oh yeah. It'll be fine. You know me. I have a list of cab companies and their

numbers ready to go."

I did know. Even when we were little and going on family vacations, Anne would make a list for me on what to pack, itemizing the clothing down to shirt color.

"And Mom will be here in a couple of days, and I'm sure she can shorten the dress," Anne continued, bringing me back to the present. "Listen to me, complaining to you when you're just starting your vacation. Sorry, it'll be fine, I know. You just need to get here, and I'll be better. Even talking to you is helping, so thanks, sis. I'll take a page from your book and relax a little. Now tell me more about what you and Kathleen have been doing. The reunion going well? I know how much you've missed her."

"It *has* been really nice, having her physically here to talk to and share things with. Having the same thoughts or reactions. You know how we can be!"

"Yes, I do."

I'm glad I had bought that international calling package from my cell phone service, because my sister and I could talk. We actually talked for about thirty minutes, and I was just hanging up when Kathleen came back and found me on the bench.

"How's the twin doing?"

"Great! She and James pretty much have everything set and are just trying to relax. How about you; what'd you find?"

"Well, I couldn't get into the dorm. I guess you have to be signed in now, but that's okay. It couldn't have changed that much. I *did* walk around the buildings a bit and my classrooms looked the same. No one I recognized though."

"Oh, I'm sorry."

"That's alright. It was a while ago. I was just curious."

There seemed to be more there, but I didn't push. "I could use a pint, though."

"Alrighty then! To the brewery!"

A girl happened to walk by just then and side-eyed us as she passed. We giggled and made a run for the gate. One of the Hop On Hop Off buses was just pulling up, so we bought tickets and hopped on.

# 8

I loved seeing the streets of Dublin from so high up. Kathleen and I had gone straight for the second level of the bus after boarding, excitedly marching up the stairs and only knocking into each other once during a crazy turn. I lifted my face to the sun and enjoyed the feel of the wind through my hair. In the seat across from me, Kathleen had her eyes closed and was soaking in this rare day as well.

"I don't even care when the brewery stop is," she said. "I could ride like this all day long."

We rode a few blocks in silence, taking in the architecture at eye level and looking into second-story windows. It was amazing to see the detail this high up, the scrollwork and various gargoyles. I nudged Kathleen and pointed out a particularly grotesque one.

"That building is super secure," I said.

She giggled, and we watched as some people made their way up the twisting stairs. They were more graceful than us on the ascent, but on their way to seats the driver had to brake suddenly, causing quick grabs of handrails and bodies flung into seats. I tried to hide a smile and turned away from Kathleen and her smothered laugh.

It had been such a long time since she and I had just relaxed and enjoyed time together. Over the past few years, we had spent countless afternoons listening to music or watching random reruns on MTV. Not doing much of anything but having a great time. I'd have to work on not losing that, no matter how far apart we were. Enjoying the current time seemed like a good start.

Kathleen was pointing to something and trying to get my attention. I focused on the window she indicated. The face!

"It's still here!"

Someone had made a clay sculpture of a girl's face, tongue sticking out and red hair flying behind her, and stuck it in the upper window of an abandoned-looking building. A clay pint of Guinness was sitting next to her; we could only assume in honor of the brewery in close proximity. When we had first seen her years ago it had been a bit frightening. Now we were delighted by her familiar face.

"So we're getting close then."

"I suppose we can get off," Kathleen said with a mock sigh. "We can get a much better view of this awesome day anyway."

I agreed, and we worked our way down the stairs to join the others waiting to get off at the Guinness stop.

Tickets in hand, we hurried through the line and towards the entrance to the first room of the tour. We figured we would hit the retail shop on the way out, just in case there was a Guinness item we didn't already own. Into that first room we went, with the giant pictures of grains and the harvesting on the walls. Very impressive, but having already read the signs explaining the brewing process we moved past to the giant water wall system just beyond. It was a pretty cool sight, and I was always impressed by it. Kathleen took a cheesy picture of me and we continued on.

We paused and watched the movie on Arthur Guinness and just enjoyed wandering through the familiar rooms. Watching the ingredients mix and swirl, seeing the first barrels that were used for storage, and the memorabilia that gave a real sense of what the workers experienced. Even the room with the TV ads and classic posters was a must-see, and we spent some time absorbing it—Guinness' well-known campaign with the zoo animals and their keeper, a comical character in green overalls, and the posters showing the different animals interacting with him, sometimes with hilarious results.

A particular favorite of mine was the television ad with a cartoon sea lion barking out, "Guinness is GOOD FOR YOU." Another was a poster with a lion chasing the zookeeper as he ran away carrying a pint of Guinness.

An open area with life-size sculptures of the characters caught our attention. Other visitors were taking advantage of the photo opportunity, and Kathleen and I joined in. We took turns snapping pictures of each other on a bench with the life-size zookeeper sculpture and even convinced a cute young lad to take a picture of us together. When Kathleen decided to climb into the zookeeper's lap, I figured it was time to move on. We hurried along, ignoring the looks sent our way—especially by mothers who had just told their children to not climb on the statue. Feeling satisfied with our time, we decided to head to the Gravity Bar. Liquid refreshment was calling, and getting off our feet sounded good too.

We took the stairs up, feeling in our pockets for the free pint coupon. As we entered the bar, we noticed it was fairly open, so we had our pick of seats along the window wall. The counter was starting to fill up with people waiting, but we found a spot to squeeze in. The closest bartender was talking to someone but seemed to be finishing up, so we watched and waited for him to glance our way.

As I spaced out in their direction, I studied the customer. There was something strangely familiar about him. The way his dark hair curled around his ears. I heard a little gasp from Kathleen and looked over at her—then followed her line of sight. The bartender was grinning at us. David! When the patron turned, I may have gasped a bit myself. Padraig shot us his warm smile, seeming a little pleased by our reaction.

"Coming for your free pint then?" David asked, grabbing two half-filled pint glasses and filling them the rest of the way. I automatically reached for my coupon, and he waved it away. "Keep it. You may need it when I go off shift," he said, with a knowing grin. Padraig was still smiling at me, and I tried to gather myself.

"Fancy meeting you here," I finally said. "I guess you really do come here. And you." I slid my gaze to David. "You could have said you worked here when I was going on and on last night."

"Nah, the look on your faces was too much fun. Couldn't pass it up." He laughed again and moved down the bar to help another customer.

"I don't mean to intrude on your vacation. I really do visit David here from time to time, and he talked me into this little surprise."

"Oh, don't be silly. We like these little surprises." I seemed to be settling in quite nicely. "Please join us." Kathleen nodded and led us to some window seats.

"How was the tour? And the rest of your day?"

We aimed for a group of three bucket-type swivel chairs placed in a grouping around a small, mirrored table. I raised my pint glass and said "First, let us pay homage." Padraig and Kathleen raised their glasses and with a "Sláinte" we all took a sip. It really wasn't the same back home.

I relaxed into my chair as Kathleen shared today's visit to Trinity and her memories from before. Padraig seemed genuinely interested and admitted he had once thought of studying in California. I quietly watched them both and drank my beer, feeling both content and excited, if that was possible. Quality time with my best friend and an unexpected, yet very welcome, new person pushing in.

Padraig stood up, indicating his empty glass. "I never got a chance to buy you two a drink last night. Another?" We nodded, and he walked around the cluster of seats to the bar. While he was occupied, I turned to Kathleen.

"What is happening right now?"

She just gave a little squeal and squeezed my knee. "This should certainly help you get over what's-his-name." While I didn't want to count the proverbial chickens before they hatched, at this moment I had to agree. The butterflies in my stomach right now—well, they had me a long way from old what's-his-name.

"I am not going to lose my head here. I've just met him and we're in *Ireland*. Besides, he's probably just being nice."

"Uh, okay. Well, nothing wrong with a bit of fun. And you never know—it's the kind of thing books are made from."

"Hey, we haven't even looked out the windows yet!" We stood up and shoved each other, laughing as we crowded up to the nearest set of windows and looked out. The view really was magnificent. With all the rooftops and chimneys stretching out before us, Dublin looked like a miniature city. Our faces were literally pressed to the glass as we got caught up in the scene before us. This was how Padraig found us.

I felt a presence behind my left shoulder and turned my head, seeing a third set of eyes. "What are we looking at?"

I laughed at the picture we must make. "Hey, I said we loved the view." We each took a pint glass from him, and the three of us sat back down. "So, Padraig," I said. "Tell us a bit about yourself. Did you go to school to work in the hotel industry or is the work just something for now?"

"I didn't really go to school for it, but in hotels is where I want to spend my career. I suppose I'm a bit of an apprentice right now, learning as much as I can on the job. Someday I'd actually like to have my own."

"*Really.* Isn't that interesting, Amelia?" Kathleen was looking at me suggestively, and Padraig looked back and forth between us.

"My sister and I once said it would be fun to open a B&B together," I explained.

"Well, if you ever have any questions—"

"I'll know who to ask."

Padraig smiled at that and then leaned forward. "Tell me about this sister of yours. I know she's getting married soon and the reason you two are here. What else?"

"Well, Anne and I are twins, so we're very close. She used to live here—did the same program Kathleen did, in fact, but at different times. She's a teacher in California, lives in San Francisco not far from me, went to college with Kathleen and me."

"Twins! So there are two of you running around Ireland. Well, that must be a nice relationship to have."

"Yeah, Anne's something else," Kathleen interjected. "Quite the smart aleck. These two were fun to go to school with."

"And she spent time here too? Is that how you know Ireland so well then? Little towns like Doolin."

"Yes," I answered. "Between her and Kathleen, I've explored all over. Anne and I actually had Thanksgiving dinner in Doolin—soup and brown bread anyway, in a little pub. It was great."

"Hey, what time is it?" Kathleen broke in.

Padraig checked his watch. "Just about 3:30."

"Oh!"

I was guessing she had suddenly remembered the car rental. "We have to get the car before five, huh?" I turned to Padraig. "I'm sorry to leave so quickly. We just remembered we have to pick up our rental car today before they close."

"Oh no, I understand. I'm sorry to have kept you so long."

"I've enjoyed talking to you, really. We both have." I looked over at Kathleen. "We have to grab a bus to take us back toward city centre."

"Can I offer you a lift somewhere?"

Not that I didn't trust him, but I had seen too many movies to be totally comfortable with this. "Oh, no thanks. We'll be fine. We actually like that bus."

"Ah yes, the Hop On Hop Off." He smiled at that. "Well, is there somewhere else I can accidentally bump into you two? Seeing as you are leaving tomorrow ..."

"Actually, we were thinking of going to the 51 later tonight," I said. The 51 was a pub in the same neighborhood as our B&B and a favorite in previous times.

"Really?" he said. "I know it. Well, maybe I will see you there." He walked us as far as the bar, where he took another spot at the counter near David. "Until then," he said with a little wave.

I raced down the stairs after Kathleen with Padraig's face lingering in my head. I couldn't help smiling myself. Had he really sought us out? Maybe, just maybe, something was starting to happen here.

# 9

Kathleen and I stood looking at the Hertz sign, trying to catch our breath. It was 4:30, so we'd made it with time to spare. That had been the longest bus stint we had spent. No hopping off to see the sights for us, but that was alright. The novelty of the second-level bus ride was what we had really purchased, and the weather had held beautifully. As a matter of fact, I was feeling a bit overheated at the moment from our jog (we'd made a few wrong turns trying to find the agency).

"Shall we?" I said now that I was breathing normally again.

Kathleen nodded, and we pushed open the door. The counter was empty and a lady was smiling at us from behind it, so we walked right to her. I gave her my name since I had made the reservation, and she went to work looking me up. Kathleen took the time to sit on a cushy bench seat against the window and leaned her head back. Guess she was still a little winded.

"Sorry, I'll just need you to fill out some paperwork but we'll bring the car around."

I jumped and turned back to the lady, grinning a bit sheepishly. She seemed pleasant enough though, and even suggested Kathleen go outside to check out the car while I filled everything out to save us time. Kathleen hopped up and did just that. I finished filling out the necessary insurance information and signing waivers that I wouldn't take the car off-roading and walked out to find Kathleen staring at the car.

"Hmm ... a bit smaller than we expected," I finally said.

She turned and looked at me. "I know cars here are more compact, but I don't think my suitcase will even fit in the backseat much less the trunk!"

"Fuel-efficiency is nice, but if we're sitting on our suitcases …"

We stood looking at the tiny car for a moment, then headed back inside to ask about upgrading to a "mid-size" vehicle. We were assured this was no problem (and actually quite common) and were soon on our way, much more comfortable with our suitcases tucked away in the trunk.

As Kathleen had driven here before, she hopped behind the wheel and handed me the map she had grabbed from the Hertz lobby. I took a moment to look around the car and was excited to see a disc drive in the stereo. I still preferred CDs to simply relying on my phone and had brought a surprise for Kathleen, to be revealed a bit later in the trip.

"Okay, talk to me, Goose."

"Ha ha," I said in response to the *Top Gun* reference. "Back to Baggot Court to park this guy, I suppose?"

"Sounds good."

"Oh! I didn't think to ask about parking. I guess we can park outside, and I'll run in the front door and ask at the desk? Hopefully the B&B has specific spaces."

"Too bad Padraig won't be there. You could bat your little eyes and probably get his."

I smacked her and pointed her in the direction we wanted to go. Three blocks later we had arrived, with only a few nearly side-swiped cars and yelling pedestrians in our wake. Not too shabby. I ran into the B&B, got the parking slip and directions to the guest parking area, and hopped back in the car. I wasn't sure where all the energy was coming from, but this sense of urgency seemed to have come over me. Kathleen seemed to have noticed it too and was side-eyeing me.

"Someone excited to get to the 51?" she finally asked.

Right. That could be it. It *had* been a while since I'd had feelings for anyone, and it was fun! But I certainly could not get ahead of myself. Talk about setting myself up. I smiled over at her apologetically.

"Trying not to but I guess not very well. Help me not be too silly, please."

"No, Am—I think it's cute, really. I'm the one who was encouraging you." She glanced at the map I had handed her again and yelled in triumph. "We're here! Am I good or what?"

"You *are* good. No, you're *great*!" I declared.

"It's all coming back. I love it." She was studying the narrow tunnel we had to drive through to get to the parking spaces. "Cars really fit through here?" We both held our breath as she inched us along, as if that would help us shrink down. Miraculously, not too much later we were rolling out the other end and maneuvering into a spot. We decided to ignore the faint scraping sound we heard at one point.

Back in our room, we lay on our beds, flat on our backs, enjoying being off our feet.

"Is it really only day two?" I asked the room in general.

"Umm, I think so, yes."

The jet lag and excitement were finally taking their toll. Ireland, unexpected surprises, unexpected emotions. I felt like I could lie there for days, just letting everything swirl around in my brain. A soft snore across from me told me Kathleen could too. Maybe it wouldn't hurt to close my eyes for just a moment ...

I jumped awake, trying to remember where I was. Hotel room, Kathleen snoring—right. I checked my watch to see it had only been about thirty minutes. Not too bad, though I was not helping my narcolepsy case any. Jet lag was a good excuse, but still.

I got up and walked to my bag as quietly as I could, not wanting to disturb Kathleen. Might as well pull out clothes for the evening while I had the chance. My mind drifted to Anne and wondered what she was doing right now. I smiled as I pictured her getting ready for the wedding and how happy she must be, even with the setbacks she'd mentioned earlier. She had waited for this day for so long and had always dreamed of being married in Ireland, though it had seemed too much of an extravagance. Well, here was proof that dreams really could come true. She had found an amazing guy too. I was happy for my sister, though I could not help feeling a little wistful for myself.

It had been just over a year since I had seen him, saying my final goodbye on that quiet dirt road. Months of trying to convince him to give us another try had been of no use. That closure had been necessary but still confusing. After three years together, no tears or anger—just a soft resignation. Strange how something so big in the beginning could end with such a dull thud.

"Huh? What?"

I jumped so hard I dropped the shirt I was holding. I turned to see Kathleen staring at me in confusion. "I think I was dreaming," she finally said and rolled into a sitting position. She sat there rubbing her eyes and trying to wake up. "Jet lag." Enough said.

She got up and walked over to where I was starting to change. "You okay?" she asked. "You seem quiet."

"Oh yeah," I replied. "Just thinking. Anne and James are lucky, y'know? To have found each other."

Kathleen studied me for a moment and smiled. "Yeah—they are."

"Well, our unplanned nap threw off our schedule a bit. Time is just flying! We should go soon if we want to get to Carrolls before they close."

"Oh geez, you're right. I'll change real quick, and we can go."

When she came out of the bathroom a few minutes later, we eyed each other's matching brown sweaters. She ran back into the bathroom and came out again wearing light blue. With that, we were out the door to race to Carrolls.

# 10

Carrolls had not changed a bit. They still displayed shelves upon shelves of shot glasses, playing cards, T-shirts, dolls—anything visitors to Ireland could possibly think to take home as a memory of their trip. We loved every bit of it and wandered the store to see what trinket we needed to add to our collection.

Kathleen was looking at a rack of pewter necklaces with Celtic designs, and I decided to head to the back wall of rugby jerseys. I had started to wear a hole through a seam in my current one and thought it only wise to have a backup. My St. Patrick's Day celebrations just would not be the same without one. I was making my way past a screaming child and an embarrassed mother trying to calm him down when Kathleen squeezed up behind me.

"Look at this," she cried in delight, holding out a shot glass with "Póg Mo Thóin" written across it. It also carried a picture of a donkey with a lipstick mark on its rear. "We should give it to Anne and James as a wedding present." The little boy had quieted down and was trying to see what Kathleen was holding, much to his mother's chagrin. She gave us a look and guided him away.

"That is not a wedding present," I said with a laugh, but grabbed it and added it to my purchases anyway. "Actually, it will be a nice addition to the Waterford crystal wine glasses and candlestick holders I already bought. They'll display it proudly on their dining room table."

"Well, I saw a mug too, if you think they'd like it—"

"*No.* I think this will do."

She winked and bustled away to continue her shopping. I turned my focus back to the task at hand and selected a jersey from the wall, then worked my way through the narrow aisles to a mug rack and found a fun, swirly pattern for my desk at work. A wall of dolls and whiskey-flavored chocolate caught my eye, and I went to investigate. This place really was a wonderland.

I was trying to decide between an Irish dancer doll and a Celtic angel doll when I noticed Kathleen making her way towards me, arms loaded with goodies and a leprechaun hat perched on her head. "Look at all this great stuff. I promised people I would bring back gifts."

"I would say you're keeping your promise," I said, eyeing her collection. "Who's the hat for?"

"Oh, I don't know, but someone needs it."

*Well, alrighty then.* "Shall we buy this stuff and go before we go too nuts? We do have a lot more country to see."

"You're right," Kathleen said, leading the way to the register. "Save room for some homemade shortbread or soap."

Standing outside the front door, we clutched our bags and tried to figure out our next move. Head straight to the B&B for a bag drop and then the 51? Grab a little refreshment and rest our feet a bit first? Decisions, decisions.

Rest and refreshment won out, so we made our way to Thing Mote. Our stomachs reminded us we had passed right through lunch, so we grabbed sandwiches at a little deli along the way and ate as we walked. It was just so easy being here, like a second home. Both Kathleen and Anne had thought of staying permanently way back when, and we had all thought of moving here since. Might be time to revisit that. I mean, I was happy in San Francisco and excited to finally be in a publishing house, but the excitement and *adventure* of Ireland were really grabbing hold of me. Maybe it was a bit of remembering a simpler and hopeful time, too, when the three of us had no attachments and were just dreaming of what our futures might hold.

Soon, we were back at Thing Mote and pushed through the front door as if we belonged there. Tom was behind the counter and glanced up and smiled as we walked in. I nudged Kathleen in the back as she walked ahead of me to the bar, wondering if she remembered what I had said as we were leaving yesterday. She turned and gave me a look, letting me know she did.

We grabbed stools at the bar, and I was about to order when I heard Kathleen say, "Hey!" I looked past her and saw Padraig, this time looking a little sheepish. I just laughed, feeling more delight than embarrassment.

"You are so following us!"

"I swear I'm not," he said with a laugh, palms up in submission. "I live close by so when I'm not working, this is where I come, wandering the streets of city centre." He motioned to Tom for another drink. "Plus, I know this guy." When Tom came over he ordered three shots of Jameson. "It's time to get serious, ladies."

Tom poured himself a shot as well, and we all toasted and took a swig. Tom knocked the entire thing back, which was impressive because I remember a friend doing that once and it wasn't so pretty. The rest of us placed our glasses back on the counter, preferring to savor them a bit.

Kathleen started talking with Tom about when she lived at Trinity, so I grabbed my drink and took the stool next to Padraig. "No point in talking around them," I said as I sat down. Where was this forwardness coming from? Maybe the smile Padraig was giving me helped.

"Okay, now it's your turn," he said. "Tell me about *yourself*. What do you do in California?"

"I'm a book editor. I'm actually really excited about it—I've been trying to break into the business and finally have, just recently." Why was I telling him all this? Ah, yes, the smile again.

"Oh. And what does a book editor do exactly?"

"Well, all sorts of things really. Chooses the manuscripts, makes sure the writing is grammatically correct, helps get the books printed."

"Do not let her fool you." Kathleen had leaned forward to chime in. "She's a fiend with that pen." She smiled at me, then turned back to Tom.

I laughed a little self-consciously as Padraig shot me a questioning look. "Okay, so I am really into grammar and know obscure rules. I'm constantly noticing mistakes, from billboards to restaurant menus and websites. I guess it's a bit of a hobby."

"Well, that sounds quite useful. Though now I'll watch myself and thoroughly reread any notes I write you."

He was going to write me notes? There was that heat in my face again. I tried to laugh lightly, though it might have tipped to hysterically. "Oh, please, don't let me make you nervous. It's just a weird little thing I have. Cleaning up the world, one word at a time." Wow, how cheesy was that?

"Not weird at all," Padraig countered. "Just a bit—unusual. I would say it makes you special." He held my gaze for a moment then glanced down with a hint of a smile, seemingly a bit embarrassed himself. Who *was* this guy, and where had he come from?

"Well, I'm trying to tone it down and not point things out. At least outside of work."

"And when did you decide to become an editor?" Padraig continued.

"I loved stories as a kid. Reading books, writing. In college, I really enjoyed my literature and writing classes and liked helping roommates with their essays." I took another sip of whiskey and shrugged. "It all just kind of came together."

"Your glass is getting low. Would you like something else? Bulmers perhaps?" He had noticed my drink last night!

"Yes, please, that would be great."

As he turned to get Tom's attention, I took the chance to look beyond him to Kathleen. She already had another drink in front of her and had her forearms resting on the bar, totally in conversation with Tom. He, too, was leaned in and engrossed. It made me smile to see her so happy, and I wondered what they were talking about. I'd try to find out later.

Padraig finally got Tom's attention and ordered our drinks, then leaned his head closer to me. "He's a really good guy. Known him most of my life." Oops. He must have seen me watching them, but seemed pleased I was looking out for my friend.

I figured I should make some sort of response but Kathleen turned to us, providing a timely distraction.

"What's going on down here? Any juicy secrets I've missed?"

"No. Are there juicy secrets to be told?" Padraig sounded interested.

"Well, when you've known each other as long as we have things are bound to happen," I replied with a laugh. "But you have to earn the right to those stories."

Kathleen agreed and turned back to Tom as he passed us our drinks. What *were* they talking about? A group of people walked through the doors, and one of the guys yelled to Padraig. He excused himself to say hello, and I took a moment to sip from my glass and observe the room. The pub had started to fill up while I was engrossed in conversation (his accent, more like!), and the noise level had risen a bit with groups laughing and chatting in different pockets.

A group of college-aged girls were gathered on the stage area Kathleen and I had sat at yesterday, laughing over some shared story. Oh, to be that age again, just starting that phase of adulthood and exploring ideas and interests. I envied the innocence and sense of limitless hope, though having my hard work pay off in the form of my current job was pretty satisfying as well. If I were completely honest, though, it still felt like something was missing. A sort of excitement. I'd put all my energy and attention into moving myself forward career-wise. Hmm ...

Padraig was still talking with his friends, so I indicated to Kathleen that I was going to the restroom. On the way to the narrow hallway leading downstairs to the toilets, I decided to first peek upstairs at the little loft area. Anne, especially, had had many interesting nights up here. One of my favorites was the night one of the history teachers pointed to a spot on the high stone ceiling and informed us that folks had been hung from there as punishment in medieval times. Talk about a good way to bring an entire party down instantly.

At the top of the stairs I did a bit of a double take. There was the old wrought-iron gate that served as a door to some back area, but when I looked in the room I saw not the loft but more of a separate bar. Another bartender glanced up and gave me a smile as an invite, but there were no other people in the room. Maybe they'd decided to wall it up and use it for private parties? I returned her smile and made my way back downstairs. I guess even in ancient cities things had to change every now and again. I glanced over as I headed for the other stairs and noticed Padraig moving towards the bar stools, looking this way and that as he noticed my empty seat. Better get back soon.

As I returned, Padraig was turned to say something to Kathleen and Tom and glanced over as I walked up.

"*There* she is," he said as I sat down.

"Sorry, I just had to go to the ladies'." Oh the lingo, so proper. "Where are your friends; still here?"

"No, they just popped in for a quick one. I would have introduced you, but they were late for a show. Never can plan ahead, those guys."

"That's alright. You were gracious enough to introduce us to your friends last night. Do they come here too?"

"Actually, this is a favorite of Cora and her friend Sinead's, who was supposed to join us last night. She might drop in at some point." He leaned in as if to share a secret. "She fancies Tom, but don't tell her I said that. She'll deny it," he said and gave my arm a little nudge. My heart definitely leapt a bit at the contact.

"I won't tell Kathleen, either. I haven't seen her show interest in anyone in a while, and she definitely would not want to step on anyone's toes."

Padraig nodded with some interest. "And what about you then? What is your situation?"

Were we really going here? I felt my heart speed up. "I'm single. No one of particular interest at home, but I'm open to it."

"Ah, so you are playing it cool then," he teased me.

"I don't mean to be playing anything," I replied with some nervous laughter as I felt a flush starting. "And what about you, since we're digging in?"

"Hit with my own question." He laughed. "Fair enough. Single as well. Ended a relationship a couple years ago and been focusing on work."

"And do you and the guys go trolling the pubs each weekend looking for women?"

That got another laugh out of him.

"No! Trolling? What kind of expression is that—American slang?"

I laughed with him. "Well, I'm not sure how many people actually say it. Anne and I may have made it up."

"They do that a lot," Kathleen chimed in, leaning around Padraig's shoulder. I guess she had lost Tom's undivided attention with the room filling up. "Anyone still want to go to the 51?"

"That's right. I was supposed to accidentally bump into you two there," Padraig said.

I smiled and checked my watch. "It's almost ten o'clock! Wow, time flies." *When you're talking to a cute Irishman.* "I'm okay not going. It was more Anne's place, anyway."

"And with getting on the road tomorrow, we can have a couple more here and then head back to get a good sleep," Kathleen added.

"Seamus won't be *too* disappointed."

"Seamus?" Kathleen looked at Padraig.

"He works there when he's not playing gigs. His dad owns the place."

"Well, aren't you just the lucky one? Friends spread strategically around the city," I said, with a laugh.

"Well, I've basically grown up with the group you met last night. We all stayed in service industries and just stuck together. It's a nice network, actually."

I found myself envying this idea, having felt a bit alone in my pursuit of writing and editing. How great to have professional supports that also happened to be good friends. There was something to that.

"Cora didn't tell you that last night," Padraig was saying. *Oops, better tune back in.* "She was too busy making fun of Seamus, but yeah. She'll get up and sing with the band every now and again. Quite a voice too."

"Why doesn't she do it more often or pursue it as a career?" Kathleen asked.

"She saw how much fun I was having with the hotel and had to do it too," he said, with a chuckle. "She actually works at a place connected to a pub and sings there sometimes. There's an open mic night and karaoke, so she gets the guests and locals into it. I think she would like to own a place like that someday."

"Really?" Kathleen leaned towards me and raised her eyes suggestively.

"Right ... you have an interest in this as well," Padraig said to me. *What was I saying about that support network? Weird.*

"It had just been kind of a fun thought, especially as my sister and I had frustrations at work. We love to travel and what a great way to be part of that world." I shrugged. "We even have our mom and Kathleen into it, a whole family affair. We'll see—maybe one day."

Just then we heard a bit of a ruckus at the front door and turned to see Cora walking in with some friends. I had just met her last night but found myself smiling and happy to see her. She saw us and came over, giving out hugs and kisses on the cheek as if we were old friends. A thin girl with long, straight brown hair trailed after her. Cora introduced her as Sinead, and we started sharing stories of what had happened in her absence the night before. She seemed very warm and funny, and we got on just as quickly as we had with Cora.

The other girls from their group had disappeared so they joined us. We ordered another round of drinks (I swore I saw Cora eye Tom and blush) and continued an easy banter late into the night. By the time we parted ways to head back to the B&B, Kathleen and I found we had made some great new friends and were a bit sad to think of leaving Dublin the next day. But we'd exchanged phone numbers, and you just never knew where things could go.

# 11

The countryside was even more beautiful than I remembered. The lush green hills rolling along gently next to us, the craggy bushes that stuck out into the road here and there, the mossy rock walls that looked like magical things should live in them. Next to me Kathleen had a perma-smile on her face, so I knew she was enjoying it, too. We'd been on the road for about thirty minutes and were heading south towards the Wicklow Mountains, relying on a map and Kathleen's memories. She'd volunteered for the first leg, allowing me to take in the scenery and think on the morning.

We'd eaten breakfast early and hung outside in the garden area for a bit, then gone back to the room to pack up before check-out time. I didn't think I had waited until the last minute to extend time with Padraig, but what can I say. I was a girl on vacation, smitten by an accent, and had not felt that way in a long time. Kathleen never commented or complained, but she did keep grinning at me.

Padraig had bid us farewell with a "have fun" and "good journey." He'd even given us brief hugs (maybe he did that for all the guests?) but knew he would see us again in a week as we had rebooked for a night to end our trip in Dublin. He'd been upbeat enough but seemed not as warm. Maybe it was my imagination. I'd only met him two days ago, so why did I feel like I had left a little something behind? I felt eyes on me and glanced over to find Kathleen looking at me.

"I thought you'd fallen asleep," she said, with a laugh.

"That would be my way, wouldn't it?" I replied. "No, just getting lulled by the road." I sat up in my seat. "That's better. Time to wake up. Oh!" I remembered the CD I'd made for our trip and reached into my bag. "It's time for *this*," I said triumphantly and waved the disc in front of Kathleen.

"Well, where did that come from?" she asked, looking around the car. "Did you make us one of your mix CDs?"

"Surprise!" I exclaimed with delight. "I made us a trip CD to increase our road trip enjoyment. Get ready ..."

I popped the disc into the stereo unit and sat back, trying to remember which song would come first. The driving beat of "The Distance" by Cake came blaring out of the speakers.

"Good driving music! To think of all the times we've listened to this over the years," Kathleen said.

We started singing along, and Kathleen tried not to take the winding turns too quickly in her excitement. Next came Josh Groban's voice crooning out "Vincent," and we both settled back down. Now this was music to enjoy a mellow drive through beautiful countryside. When No Doubt's "Just a Girl" came on, Kathleen said, "This is one random CD."

I had also thrown in some Enya and U2 for good measure. With the sounds of "Only Time" in the background, I decided to get a little serious. "So, you seemed a little quiet when we were at Trinity. Were you okay?"

"Yeah!" Kathleen looked at me with surprise, then relented a bit. "I just miss it, y'know? All the good memories, living in the city ... I got a little thoughtful, I guess."

"Yeah, I hear you. Those were some fabulous times." I had not meant to get too heavy but sighed a bit as I looked out the window.

"Are you happy, Am?"

Now it was my turn to give her a surprised look. "Sure." Then I smiled apologetically. "It's just so good to be with you like this. It's making me a little nostalgic too. I miss it," I said, turning to face my friend.

When Kathleen hit the brakes, I was completely blindsided. The car jarred to a stop and I had to spin forward before my ear hit the windshield. I threw my hand over my heart and forced my eyes to focus on the sheep facing us in the middle of the road. This was actually quite common, but we'd been too caught up in our conversation to pay attention. The sheep continued to chew on whatever he (or she) was eating and looked at us with mild interest as the rest of the flock trailed around the corner.

We had to work hard to squelch the hysterical laughter trying to bubble over, but we managed a polite smile and wave to the sheepherder as he came up behind his flock and moved them past us. Once they had moved down the road, we finally let it out.

"Dude!" I exclaimed. "That was crazy!"

Kathleen was doubled over and finally caught her breath. "I almost hit a *sheep*! That scared me so bad!"

We gathered ourselves and continued down the road—at a much slower pace, I noticed.

"I could stretch my legs," I said, after a while. "Want to find a place to pull over and get out?"

"Sure."

We found a nice pullout with a view of the hills, and Kathleen eased the car off the road. The breeze felt wonderful on my cheeks, and I watched as my friend carefully climbed down across some rocks. I followed after her and chose a longer yet easier route, enjoying the feel of the spongy grass under my feet.

"This is marvelous," she said softly, almost reverently, and turned to me with a big grin on her face.

"It sure is. Yeah ... I could get used to this," I said, on a sigh.

Kathleen had settled on a large, moss-covered rock and I dropped down beside her. She stared ahead in silence for a few moments. I joined her and took in the view. It was too beautiful not to. The sky was a soothing light blue and the rolling hills seemed to spread endlessly before us in a grassy sea of various shades of green, broken up periodically by rocks and boulders scattered about. I felt myself relax even more.

"I still can't believe we're here," she finally said. "I know I keep saying that, but—"

"No, I agree. It *is* pretty surreal. Both of us finally being in a place where we can do this after talking about it for so long."

We continued to sit with our thoughts, and I found mine turning to Anne. I was just so happy she was finally getting her fairy tale ending and couldn't help smiling, picturing how excited she must be. I also hoped she wasn't stressing too much about the dress and transportation issues. My sister definitely prided herself on being prepared and well planned.

The sound of gravel crunching under tires made me look behind us up the hill. A car was stopping behind ours, and we decided to continue on and let them have the spot to themselves. They looked to be a couple, and we exchanged smiles and nods as we passed.

"How cute were they?" Kathleen commented as we settled back in the car. "All romantic and on a drive, getting to see that view together." Kathleen sighed. "I want a boy."

"You and me both, honey!" We laughed, and Kathleen started the car and pulled back out into the road.

"Hey—Glendalough!" I think I had scared Kathleen, but she was able to focus on the sign I was pointing to. "Anne talked about going there and how beautiful it was. The scenery and ruins—early Christianity stuff."

"Neat! Sounds good to me." Her stomach gave a rumble. "Maybe lunch wouldn't be a bad idea, either."

We both laughed and started to watch for signs.

Kathleen's stomach won out, so we stopped at a nice-looking pub on the way into a town called Laragh. We walked into a room with dark wood walls, wooden floor, and a host of curious glances thrown our way. We smiled politely and made our way to the bar, the best place to start in a new establishment. When the bartender made his way over, we asked about ordering. He handed us two menus and said he would be back.

"You're American." I looked up from my menu to smile at the gentleman sitting on the barstool next to me. "Long way from home."

"I'm here visiting with my friend," I said and Kathleen leaned around me, giving a little wave.

"Small place you found here," he said with a chuckle. "Brian, by the way," he added, and offered me his hand.

"Amelia, and this is Kathleen," I replied, clasping his hand in return. "My sister lived in Dublin for a while and loved this area, so we had to see for ourselves."

"Smart girl. Is she still here?"

"Well, she *is* actually, in Doolin. She's getting married there, which is why we're here."

"Oh, that's brilliant."

"Yeah, we're excited. I get to be the maid of honor," I finished gleefully. Why was I sharing so much with a stranger? The warmth in his eyes, the way they crinkled when he smiled, were just pulling me right in.

Kathleen had grabbed the menus and claimed a table for us, so I figured I should join her.

"I suppose we should order our lunch now," I said apologetically. "Lay a foundation before we start on the Bulmers."

He laughed. "Thanks for the chat, darlin'."

He turned back to his friend, and I heard them talking as I made my way towards Kathleen.

"He was so nice!" I think I was gushing but couldn't help it.

"I'm glad," she shot back with a laugh. "I wasn't so sure at first."

"Oh, you know these quieter places. Wary of stupid tourists bungling in."

"Remember the couple in that one town? All dressed in their brand-new, designer label outdoor gear coming into that small pub to use the restroom?"

"And that guy on the bar stool side-eying them as they walked past, all hurried and nervous? I think the lady even used a tissue to open the door," I finished with a shake of my head. "That was pretty funny."

"Some people just give tourists a bad name," Kathleen agreed.

"Okay, down to business," I said. "Food." I skimmed the menu and grinned. "Oh, who am I kidding. Shepherd's pie."

"I'm going to try the fish and chips," Kathleen replied, arching her eyebrow at me. "They *do* have other food here."

"I know. It's just so good. Hits all the food groups."

We both laughed. "I'll give you a bite of mine," Kathleen offered.

"And you *know* you'll want a bit of mine," I countered. She shrugged and nodded in agreement.

I was about to head to the bar to place our orders when I saw the bartender making his way towards us holding two pint glasses.

"Courtesy of the old guy at the bar," he said with a twinkle in his eye as he placed the drinks on the table.

Kathleen looked at me in question, and I turned to see Brian smiling at us. He raised his glass to us and we raised ours in return and took a sip. Bulmers! The bartender was still standing there and watching us expectantly, so I placed our food order.

"Well, aren't you just making friends with the locals," Kathleen said into her glass as I turned back from smiling at Brian again.

I sensed a bit of a tone and frowned slightly, wondering about it. What was this about? Just my imagination?

"What?" I finally asked.

"Oh nothing," she said. "When I lived here it just seemed the locals were not so friendly towards outsiders, that's all."

"Oh, well ..." I wasn't sure where to go with that. "I'm glad we changed these guys' minds," I said lightly, trying to move past the tension.

Kathleen seemed lost in thought for a few moments, then came back with a slight shake of her head. She smiled at me, almost shyly. I smiled in return, relieved. Best not to touch it. Kathleen had always been so confident, definitely the more balanced in our duo. I didn't want to tip the scales now, especially feeling so distant from her recently.

Our food arrived and we dug in, eating in companionable silence, relaxed once again.

# 12

We stood in the doorway of the pub and stared out, mouths open in shock. Lines of water streamed inches from our noses, and we could barely see across the parking lot from the rain bouncing so hard off the ground.

"When did this happen?" Kathleen looked at me incredulously. "It was sunny when we got here, not a cloud in the sky." We continued staring at each other, then burst out laughing.

We had finished our meal and shared another round of thanks and handshakes with Brian and his friend and were now looking to set off on our exploration of the ruins. Well, maybe not now. We exchanged a look and turned to walk back into the pub.

"Back so soon, darlin's?" Brian yelled from his barstool, then looked behind us out the door. "Well look at that. It's pissin' rain!"

"Sorry, girls," his friend said. "Looks like you won't be seeing the ruins today, unless you packed rain gear or don't mind getting a good soaking."

At our crestfallen looks, Brian was quick to chime in. "Find a place to stay here for the night. This is a lovely town."

I glanced at Kathleen. "We would need a place to stay the night anyway. Might be nice to slow down and hole up for a while. Definitely better than driving those roads in the rain."

"You're right, and that does sound nice. Know any good places?" She turned to Brian.

"Sure. Try Riversdale House. I know the owner; it's grand. Hey,

Gerry," he called to the bartender, "call Liam and see if he has a room for these nice girls."

Gerry nodded and grabbed the phone. A moment later, he hung up and gave us a thumbs up, walking over with a card in his hand. There was a map on the back showing us how to get there, and it was not far at all.

"Liam's ready for you and excited for some new faces. Says he'll have hot chocolate ready," the bartender said with a grin.

"Thank you guys, so much."

"Yes, that was really nice," Kathleen added, giving a big smile. "I can't wait to see this place."

"There looks to be a little break in the weather, so better go now," Brian advised.

We gave another wave and headed out the door. It *had* lightened up considerably, but Kathleen offered to drive again so this weather wasn't my first experience behind the wheel here. I was not arguing with that.

We had only driven a short while when Kathleen spotted the small road the bartender had indicated and turned down onto it. Where was this leading us? We descended fairly steeply, winding through bushes and trees. The driving rain made it particularly exciting.

We came to a creek at the bottom of the incline and turned left, following the road until we saw the sign for Riversdale House. Kathleen turned into the graveled drive and found a spot in the small lot next to the house. We looked with delight at the building standing before us, looking so quaint and strong and warm. It appeared to have two levels and a front area made entirely of glass.

A light burning just above the front door looked very welcoming and we grabbed our bags, wanting to get there as quickly as possible. The rain had picked up again, and that hot chocolate was calling our names. We ran to huddle under the overhang on the front stoop, and the big front door opened immediately.

"You must be Amelia and Kathleen. Come in. Come in."

We hurried through the door and turned to greet our host. A nice-looking, middle-aged gentleman stood before us, with graying hair and kind, amused eyes. He wore a thick, cable-knit sweater and cords, looking every bit the proprietary country innkeeper. I could not help smiling back at him.

"I am Liam," he said, extending his hand. "I'm happy to have you."

We both shook his hand, and I took a moment to survey the entryway as Kathleen moved into conversation about the gentlemen at the pub and sudden weather change. The walls were a cozy and inviting pale yellow and a light wood staircase ran along the wall behind us, leading to the second floor. Through an archway I could see a large, multi-leveled room reaching from the front of the house to the back. The uppermost level had couches and woven throw rugs for a lounging area, and the lower had multiple tables and chairs as if for an eating area.

"You girls must be ready to relax. Head on into the lounge. I have hot cocoa ready like I promised," Liam said, motioning into the room I had been studying. "Leave your bags," he said in response to our glances at our luggage. "I will take them up to your room."

We expressed our gratitude and hurried into the room to see what surprise awaited us. A tray with two steaming mugs of hot chocolate and small plates of shortbread cookies had been laid on a large coffee table that sat amidst a few plush couches. We sank onto one of the couches, delighted by this turn of events. Kathleen grabbed a cookie and turned to me with a big grin that probably matched my own.

"This is so great. Can you believe it?" She giggled and took a bite.

I raised my mug and toasted her. "Thank you, Brian." Crazy change to our day, but it was actually really nice to be sitting here, cozy and tucked in from the storm. I looked out the wall of windows to see rain streaking down even heavier than before.

"Too bad about the ruins," Kathleen said, "but now we can have a slumber party like old times. A daytime slumber party." Her eyes glinted, and she smiled.

"Maybe tomorrow we can try again," I added with a shrug. "This works for me, too." I bit into a cookie. Mmm ...

Kathleen sat back and tucked her legs under her. "Okay, friend. What can we talk about?"

I looked over at her, and it hit me again how much I had missed her. It was just so easy being in her space, comforting even. Knowing someone and sharing so many experiences over twenty years. Well, that was pretty special.

"Um ..." I said, with a smile.

"I know what you want to talk about. Or rather *who*," she said, with a wicked grin.

I couldn't help it. I giggled. "I've tried to be good," I said. "I haven't been annoying and moony, right?" She shook her head. "Good. I mean, nothing can really happen. Right?"

"I don't know." She shrugged. "Stranger things have happened . . ."

For the first time, I let the possibility really enter my thoughts. What if? The feelings had felt real enough and—different. A warmth washed over me, and I tried to push it back down.

"Uh-*huh*. You *are* thinking about it, aren't you?"

"I want to just get carried away and have fun, but I have to keep my feet on the ground a *little* bit."

"He didn't mess you up that bad, did he?"

"Who?"

"You know."

"Oh." I laughed, but wanted to answer her seriously too.

"I guess we haven't really talked much about this, huh? Now that I'm on this side of it I can." At least, I hoped I could. "At first it was really hard and confusing. I mean, if I hadn't done anything wrong why was I out of his life? And I couldn't understand how something could be so out of the blue." Remembering that phone call on the day after Christmas—telling me he was done and wanting to move out, after hinting at a proposal not even a week prior—with no sign of unhappiness in our three-year relationship. It did still sting.

"Physically ... sheesh. Sometimes I felt so light—like I was fading away or about to pass out. But it got easier. It would have been easier if *you* were there, but I think healing from something like that shows what strength a person really has."

"I bet Anne and the rest of your family were a big help, and other friends from the Bay," Kathleen added.

"Oh, for sure. Knowing others cared—it helped. Someone said to me that we can't be running away from something but have to be running towards something else, and it stuck with me. My reasons for staying diminished, so that was when I decided to move. It was tough but ended up being the best thing I could have done. And look at all that's happened since then." I smiled.

Kathleen blew out a sigh. "And you thought that maybe he had cheated, right?"

"Well, I don't know that I *really* thought that. It was just the only thing that made sense with such an instant one-eighty-degree turn. I asked him and, of course, he denied it. No one else could say for sure, either."

"You mean his family and friends?"

"Right. The few friends he had." I shrugged.

"Well, that sounds like one hell of a process. Trying to make sense out of that without any help from the person involved." She shook her head. "Thanks for sharing. I know we've talked a bit, but I wanted to give you space to work it out and move on too. You certainly are a tough cookie."

I smiled, touched, and took a bite of cookie. This was definitely a cookie-and-hot-chocolate kind of conversation.

"And I think you *definitely* deserve a fun romance on your vacation," she continued. "I don't know. I think maybe a heart has to be horribly broken before it can recognize the one who will take care of it. Not to get all deep or anything, but I've never seen you like this before. It's good," she finished, sending me a warm smile.

"Well, thanks for the vote of confidence. I *do* feel different, and it's nice. And to answer your question, *no,* he didn't mess me up. Just made me a little smarter, I guess." I shrugged again and finished my cookie, then grabbed my mug of hot chocolate.

"Hello, girls. How are we?"

I admit I jumped just a little as Liam walked into the room. I guess our conversation was more intense than I realized.

Kathleen had stood and was thanking him profusely. I set my mug down and stood too, joining the conversation.

"Your bags are all set in your room—up the stairs, turn right, the room at the end of the hallway. My best room, girls," he said. "Nice windows to see the storm if you like." He motioned upward. "You're welcome to head up or stay here, does not matter to me. I'll be in my office doing some work if you need anything." With a nod, he turned and left the room.

"Are you thinking room?" I asked Kathleen.

She nodded, and we gathered our sweaters and tray of goodies. (There were actually some cookies left). I couldn't wait to really settle in and get comfortable.

# 13

The upstairs felt very airy, with plush off-white carpeting and crisp, white walls. Plants and small statues were placed on shelves here and there and slanted windows that seemed part skylight ran the length of the hallway, letting in wonderful views of the back hillside. They were now fairly darkened and rain-streaked, but I'm sure on sunnier days it was beautiful.

Kathleen used the key to open our door and—wow. Big wood beams criss-crossed the ceiling and our feet sank into more plush carpeting. Two beds ran along opposite walls with fluffy white duvets and cozy, plaid blankets. A small, light-colored wood writing desk and chair were tucked into a corner with a charming lamp on top, and we looked to have our own bathroom. Yeah, I could spend some time here.

We unpacked quickly into a small chest of drawers, just a few things to feel more settled in, and I changed into sweats. Now it was cozy time. Kathleen agreed and did the same. In no time we were sitting cross-legged on our cushy beds with the rest of our hot chocolate and cookies in front of us. I couldn't keep the goofy grin off my face. This was just so perfect.

"*So*, Miss Maid-of-Honor. Thought of your toast yet?" Kathleen asked between cookie bites.

"Oh right. Should I do the traditional one Anne and I found?"

"You mean with the downing of the whiskey and slamming the glass onto the floor? Definitely."

"I've always wanted to. Hmm ..." How would that go over? I

would have to think on it some more.

"Speaking of ... which dress did she decide on?"

"*That* was random," I said with a laugh. "Um. I'm not sure actually." At the bridal shop in San Francisco, we had all gathered as my sister tried on dress after dress, finally narrowing the choices down to three. Anne had wanted more time to think on it and surprise us all with her final choice. We had tried on bridesmaid dresses as well, and found some that worked well and came in an array of colors—some better than others. She was surprising us with this as well.

"Huh. She wouldn't even tell her twin. Curious. "

"Yes, indeed ..."

We both twirled imaginary moustaches and cracked up. Oh my. Now the sillies were setting in.

"Hey!" Kathleen suddenly sat up and looked out the window. "Do you hear that?"

"What?"

"Silence. I think the rain has let up!"

"Oh, yeah! Want to explore before it starts up again?" The sky still looked pretty dismal.

"Absolutely. Grab a sweatshirt and let's ask our friend Liam if there are any good hikes around here."

We headed downstairs and did just that. We found Liam in his office just as he had said, and he was all too happy to give us some tips. It sounded like just across the creek was a flat sort of walking trail, and in either direction were cool ruins and pretty scenery to see.

"There are big rocks to cross the stream on, but mind your step. They can be a bit slippery when the water is high, as it is today, and just last month a young lady fell in. Poor girl. I think she was snockered, but wet and unhappy just the same."

We tried not to laugh too much and thanked him. Once outside we took deep breaths.

"My *gosh,* do you smell that!"

"This place really is too beautiful for words," Kathleen agreed. "Especially after a refreshing rain."

The tall trees surrounding us were an even deeper green than before and glistening a bit. The air was fresh and the clean grass smell was almost overpowering. We made our way across the narrow, rocky lane and found the path of stones leading across the creek, just past a small wrought-iron gate indicating the property line. The water seemed higher and faster after the rain, so I understood Liam's warning.

"Here goes," I said, trying to be brave as I stepped on the first stone. A little slick, but not too bad. The water was not quite to the tops of the rocks, so we didn't have to worry about wet shoes. Well, hopefully. I placed my foot on the second, then third rocks.

Kathleen yelled from behind me, "Don't fall!"

Gee, thanks.

"I would turn around and glare at you, but then I probably would."

She snickered. Two more *careful* steps and I was successfully across. I turned and gestured as in *your turn.* She cautiously stepped on the first rock, then the others, with no problem at all.

"Well, aren't you just proud of yourself," I said, and linked my arm through hers. "Let's go this way," I continued, and tugged her to our right.

We walked in silence for a while, just taking in our surroundings. This really was a magical place, and so peaceful. The only sounds were the crunching of the pebbles under our feet and the water flowing on our right.

My thoughts slipped to home. I loved my flat in San Francisco (and my roommate Mr. Britches, a mischievous fluffy black cat) and could not help smiling at the thought of my job and recent accomplishments there. So why did I feel like something was missing or at least like I was ready for another level. Oh, who was I kidding. I knew what was missing. I thought of Padraig and smiled again. That little heart flutter was what I was missing. Hmm ...

Next to me Kathleen sighed. I turned to her and tilted my head in question. She side-eyed me, grinning. "You heard that, huh?"

"Yes. You okay?"

"Honestly? Not really," she replied. "I don't want to get too heavy, but being here—I'm just not that happy at home anymore, Am."

"What?" I looked at my friend, waiting for further explanation and wondering how I had missed this. We really had drifted apart, in spite of our best efforts.

"Oh —just —I don't know. Everything!" She laughed, but the sound was a bit strained. "That town is just feeling—stale—and I'm not happy in my job anymore. I just want to be excited by something again." She gave me a rueful look.

"Well ... " I started, not quite sure what to say, "life is too short to settle. Maybe you *do* need a change. Move to the city with me!"

She gave me a look. "I don't know. What would I do?"

"Anything," I replied, warming to the idea. "Are you kidding? It's San Francisco! You could ... be a ferry boat pilot ... or some big wig in the Financial District. Bartend at Foley's and give me free cider!"

We both laughed, and it broke the tension a bit.

"I know it's a lot to think about and something you need to figure out. I'm glad you shared with me, though, and sorry I didn't pick up on it sooner. That must have been hard to come to. Does your family know or suspect?"

She sighed again and shook her head. "No, and how do I tell them? We spend so much time together and I love it, I really do. Sometimes I wonder if that's all I really have, or why I'm still in that small town." She turned to me, looking sad and a bit distraught, and then laughed at herself. "What am I *doing*? We're in *Ireland*."

"You're giving your brain the space to think and dream and consider other things."

"Well, enough of that. Back to the moment. I'll think on that stuff later. Look!"

I looked to where she was pointing and, sure enough, we had managed to find some ruins. Just off the path sat what appeared to be the remains of a small cottage or church. We walked towards the rectangular plot of crumbling stone, feeling a bit like trespassers. Even the birds seemed to have quieted for the moment. How cool.

A drop hit my face and next to me Kathleen wiped something off her cheek. She cast a concerned look to the skies. They were darkening again, and the wind had picked up.

"I guess that's our cue," I said. "Nice we got this reprieve, but looks like we better hustle back."

Kathleen nodded and we turned to walk back the way we had come. An older couple was strolling towards us, also enjoying an evening walk. I wondered if they were staying at our B&B or lived nearby.

I glanced at Kathleen in time to see her step on an acorn, spin on one foot, and land flat on her back. As I stared in shock, the couple rushed up in alarm.

"Oh, dear! Is she alright? Did she faint?" the woman said as she stopped at my side. The gentleman was already bending down to get a closer look.

Kathleen was staring straight up, probably wondering about the strange faces looking down at her. I snapped out of it and bent down to help her up as well. Thankfully, she was more embarrassed than hurt.

"That did not need to happen," she finally said, with a bit of a smile on her face.

She assured the couple she was okay and thanked them for their concern and help. With a final nod and "Good evening" they continued up the path, and Kathleen took a moment to gather herself. While she straightened her clothing, I tried to bite back a smile and looked anywhere else but at her. She finally giggled—and that was it.

The flood gates opened, and I doubled over laughing. She joined me and soon we were holding on to each other, gasping for breath. Fat rain drops landing on us finally brought us back. We gathered ourselves and took off at a run down the path, giggling and snickering here and there. We made it across the creek without further incident and reached the front door of the B&B just as the skies opened up.

# 14

I sat cross-legged on my bed facing Kathleen with my hands wrapped around a steaming mug of tea. The laughter had subsided, and we were happy to be warm and relaxing back in our room while the storm raged outside. Liam had been gracious enough to fix us the tea while we changed into dry clothes.

"I wonder how long this storm will last." Kathleen's voice was a bit muffled as she leaned into our closet to hang her sweaters. She turned to get my response and gave a small smile. "It's exciting and I love being cozy inside for a while. I just wonder how driving will be and when we can really be outside."

"Hmm … good point," I replied and stretched out on my stomach. "If we need to make adjustments, we can. I am really enjoying this place and having time to relax. I could stay here another day or two."

"Knock, knock!"

We both turned to see Liam approaching our open doorway.

"How are we, girls?"

"Actually, we were just saying how relaxed we are right now and could stay a while," I answered, standing up and walking to the door.

"Well, you may not be too far off. I was just watching the news, and the weatherman said this is a big one and isn't going anywhere."

Kathleen had joined us, and we just stared at each other. This was *not* the way we had imagined our trip through the countryside, but this was also one of the best places I could imagine being.

"Um, do you have open rooms tomorrow night should we need

it?" I finally asked.

"Of course, girls," he replied, smiling. "It is yours, if you want it." He paused and looked down as if he wanted to say something, then looked back up and smiled again. "I will leave you to your evening."

He turned and retreated down the hallway as I closed the door and Kathleen went back to the closet.

"What a turn, huh?" I said as I sat back down on my bed. "Changes our touring time a bit, but listen to the rain on the windows. So neat." I'm sure I sounded totally Pollyanna but couldn't help it. "I can just picture how green and sparkling things will be in the morning."

Kathleen turned and arched an eyebrow at me. I gave her a big cheesy grin back, then got up and joined her at the closet. She'd set her phone to play music, and we danced around the room while putting clothes away.

"We're such dorks," she said, a little breathless from a particularly inspired bit of hip shaking.

"Yes, we are!" I replied, quite proud of myself.

"Okay, that's enough of that." Kathleen had finished unpacking and fell onto her bed. "What are we going to do for dinner? I don't think we'll be driving back to the pub."

"You're right. Hmm ... Maybe we can ask Liam. He might have some ideas. Pizza delivery down the treacherous mountain road?"

"I'm starting to get hungry. Are you ready to head down now?"

"Start the quest for food? Absolutely. I think I burned off my shepherd's pie laughing at you earlier."

She made a face and threw a pillow at me, then grabbed a sweater and headed for the door. I followed, giggling again at the memory. We found Liam in the living room, straightening some magazines on a table. He turned at our footsteps.

"Hello, girls! Needing a bit of entertainment?"

"Actually, we were thinking of dinner and wondering if you have any suggestions," I replied.

"Ah, I am one step ahead of you. The missus is already working on a stew if that's alright. There is no coming or going in this weather."

Kathleen and I both nodded enthusiastically and thanked him. I couldn't believe how nice Liam was. Well, I guess I could, but still. What a treat.

Liam said food would be ready in about thirty minutes, so we decided to relax in the living room area. Kathleen ran back to the room to grab some postcards she had purchased in Dublin and my journal (there were some very important thoughts to record!), and joined me on one of the couches. She handed me the journal and started addressing her cards.

"Who are you writing?" Curiosity got the better of me.

"My nephews," she murmured, as she began writing.

"Oh, what a nice aunt. They'll have fun bringing those to show-and-tell."

I took my pen out of its flap and got to my own work. I couldn't help first reading my past entries, and it was amazing to see what a different place I was in than even six months ago.

So sad, comfort gone ... How is this a good thing?? ... SO MANY QUESTIONS ... What have I done to deserve this? ... Just kind of wondering what I'm missing ... MY GAWD when will this get easier ...

Man, that was hard to read, and it even seemed like another person talking. I was happy to be in my current place, and now on to the writing.

So ... Padraig. Is this crazy? I can't stop thinking about him, but is this just a vacation crush? Safe and fun, because it can't go anywhere? Or is that why I'm so hesitant? Because I don't want it to be just that. San Francisco ... I'm finally hitting a stride and so happy there. Long distance relationship from two coasts? Two CONTINENTS? I don't see him moving to California any time soon, and Ireland is awesome, but I don't see how I can call it home. And listen to me, this IS crazy.

I'm already marrying us off! Settle down, Am!

I looked up to see Kathleen peeking over my shoulder, trying to read what I was writing. "Hey!" I yelled, with a laugh.

"You were furrowing your brow and writing so ferociously. I got curious," she replied, raising her eyebrows in mock innocence.

"Oh, just being a wacko and getting ahead of myself. Promise me, you will watch me," I said, with some seriousness. "I don't want to be stupid."

She could tell I was serious. "Okay," she said, nodding. Then she gave my knee a reassuring pat and got up to stroll towards the windows. She looked outside for a bit, hands clasped behind her back, then turned to me with a small grin.

"I think things are changing for us, Am—in a good way. I really do."

I closed my journal, stood up, and walked over to stand with her. The rain continued to streak down the windows. It was soothing.

"I'm thinking you're referring to our earlier conversation? Thinking more about what else you want to do?"

"Yeah. I think you were right ... getting a little distance, mentally and physically, to let myself really think about things. I don't know what it is, but this has been the best I've felt. Living here before, being here now. I need to think more on this."

"Maybe you could reconnect with some professors at Trinity. Be a teaching assistant. Or be a barback and give me cider!"

She looked at me and smiled. "You and your cider."

We heard a noise behind us and turned to see Liam walking through the living room entrance carrying a large tray with several bowls on it.

"Are we hungry? Here we go—hot off the stove."

A woman walked into the room after him, with brown hair tied back in a bun and kind eyes that crinkled at the corner as she smiled. She wiped her hands on a towel hanging off her shoulder, then clasped each of our hands in turn.

"And this is Louise, the missus I mentioned," Liam continued, nodding his head toward her. "Couldn't keep her in the kitchen."

"Oh you!" Louise swatted her husband with the towel and chuckled. "Such a charmer. I was excited to meet our newest guests. Enjoying your stay, loves?"

"This place is beautiful," I said, while nodding enthusiastically. "And such a perfect respite from the rain that surprised us today. We're so happy Brian recommended you and connected us."

"Brian! That rascal. How's he doing?" She turned to glance at Liam. "Seems like I haven't seen him around much recently."

"Ah, who knows with that one," Liam answered and adjusted the tray, getting a better grip. "That new job of his. What's he doing again? Well, seems to keep him travelling a bit."

"Anyway," Louise continued and focused back on us. "Now, what's your story girls? Liam hasn't told me a thing."

"I was giving them their privacy."

She looked at him a moment, then turned to us again. "Where are you from? And what brings you to Ireland?"

Liam let out an exasperated—and exaggerated—sigh. We laughed. She ignored him.

"We're from California—northern to be specific," I answered. "My sister is getting married in Doolin, and we're making our way while enjoying a road trip together. Taking the scenic route."

"Yeah, you're a bit off course. Well that sounds just great.'" She sounded truly excited. "How fun you landed at our place here. I'm so glad."

Kathleen's stomach growled and we all laughed.

"That's our cue." Louise said and gestured us to a nearby table. "We'll let you eat while the stew's nice and hot."

"And this tray's not getting any lighter," Liam grumbled, but we could tell he was only joking.

Louise made her exit and we followed Liam to a nearby table, then watched as he started placing the food. Steaming bowls of stew, sliced brown bread, mushy peas, pats of butter. Now *my* stomach growled.

"Anything else I can get you, girls?"

"Oh, this is wonderful. Thank you so much, Liam," I said, as Kathleen and I sat down.

Liam turned and left the room, and we both reached for a slice of bread.

"It's warm!" Kathleen cried with delight.

I spread on some butter and took a bite. "Mmm, now that is brown bread." I dipped it in the stew and took my next bite of heaven. "This is so much better than any restaurant. Nothing like home cooking."

Kathleen nodded in agreement and kept digging into her food. Dinner could not have come at a better time. We ate in silence for quite a while, enjoying our meal and the pitter pat of the rain on the glass ceiling above us.

We were sitting on what looked to be a patio that had been attached to the house and enclosed by glass walls. The floor was made of wide, rust-brown tiles, and potted plants were scattered around the room. This would be a great breakfast nook in the morning, especially if the sun was out.

Between bites, we caught up a bit on things that had been happening at home. More work talk, her family, my family. There wasn't much we hadn't already covered, but it was different talking in person. I laughed like I hadn't in a while, and it just felt good. It was nice to have the room to ourselves, too. *Where were the other guests?* We didn't feel like we had to hold anything back or even be ladylike necessarily. Boy, had I missed this.

"Okay, I can't eat another bite," Kathleen announced and pushed back from the table. My jeans were feeling a little snug in the waist as well.

"I wonder if we leave the plates here. Feels like we should clean up after ourselves," I said, starting to gather up silverware.

"Oh, leave that," Liam said, rushing into the room. "I will get it."

Question answered.

I thanked Liam again and asked where Louise was to thank her as well. He informed us she was already making preparations for breakfast, but he'd pass our enjoyment along. We shared "good nights" and Kathleen and I made our exit, heading towards the stairs.

I glanced around the entryway again, trying to determine where the kitchen might be in case I could pop in to say good night to Louise as well. No luck, so I followed Kathleen up the stairs to our room. Once inside, she turned the music back on and flopped onto her bed, lying on her back.

"Oh, that was so good," she said. "I just want to lie here in my food coma."

"Here's to that."

The rain was still beating on the roof and was even hitting the side window now. Shifty winds.

"So tomorrow," Kathleen continued. "If there happens to be a break in the rain, do you want to try and head out or enjoy staying here?"

"I say we try and head out. It would be nice to see someplace else if we have the chance."

"I agree." She paused for a moment, then said, "This is going to sound dumb, but I kind of miss having a TV."

I laughed. "No, I agree. It would be nice to have a show to space out on right now."

"Liam said he had been watching the news. Where's his?" Kathleen said with a wicked grin.

"Probably in his private area—where his *family* lives."

"Ah, true. Don't want to freak out the kids with two strange girls joining them for evening TV."

We both laughed at the picture.

"Anyhoo," Kathleen said. "If we can leave tomorrow, where should we go? I know you've already been to Blarney Castle, and I don't really *need* to see it. I wanted to kiss the stone and all but would rather continue on towards Doolin, maybe see what's between here and there."

"Okay. Well, I really would like to visit Graiguenamanagh. I've heard it is really popular for music. Lots of bands go through there."

"Wow, say that ten times fast." Kathleen replied, with a laugh. "That sounds great. I love the music!"

"Fingers crossed then." I stifled a big yawn and realized how tired I was. "What time is it?"

"It's a little past nine. Wow, time flies."

"I could actually crawl into bed right now. Get a good night's sleep for whatever awaits us tomorrow?"

"That does sound good," Kathleen agreed, stifling her own yawn.

"I passed it!" I yelled with delight. Usually, she was good at doing that to me.

"Yes, you did." She eyed me accusingly. "You can go first if you like, since you yawned first."

"Great, thanks. Suddenly, I can hardly keep my eyes open."

I took my toiletry bag to the bathroom and cleaned off the day as fast as I could. With all the weather and different conversations, I was exhausted and bedtime would feel really nice. I came hurrying out to give Kathleen her turn and found her fast asleep, still on her back but under the covers. Guess someone was more tired than she realized. I figured it best not to wake her but leave her be.

# 15

I rolled over onto my back and stretched lazily. What a great sleep. I popped an eye open and peeked across the room at Kathleen. She, too, was starting to rouse.

"Is that bacon I smell?" she murmured blearily.

"We can only hope," I answered on a yawn.

We got out of bed, threw on sweats, and made our way downstairs to investigate. Sure enough, breakfast was in full swing and there were a few people seated at tables in the patio area. So there *were* others staying here.

Liam was holding court, walking amongst the tables and chatting here and there. He turned and saw us, greeting us with a big smile.

"Here are the girls! Good morning!"

We smiled back at him, a bit embarrassed as heads turned to look at us, and quickly sat at the nearest table. Kathleen spotted a coffee pot and mugs on a side table and made a beeline. She came back with two steaming mugs and milk for me (I really couldn't handle coffee black) as Liam started towards us. She took a sip and closed her eyes in contentment. *Now* Kathleen could start the morning.

"Good sleep, girls?"

"Yes, wonderful," I replied with a smile. "I love sleeping to the sound of rain."

"Oh, I do too. A girl after my own heart!" He seemed to be addressing the room at large, and a few people smiled and nodded. Did they all know each other?

"So would you both like the full breakfast offering?" he continued. "We serve the full Irish breakfast and waffles should you like."

"Oh, yes, please." Kathleen and I said in unison and laughed. I could get used to this, but I didn't know if my waistband could.

Liam chuckled with us and moved off to take care of our order. I added milk to my coffee and toasted Kathleen, then took a sip. Good stuff.

For getting such a full and long sleep, I was feeling pretty groggy. Kathleen seemed prone to the space-out too. I glanced around the room to see who was dining with us. A younger couple, maybe on their honeymoon from the goo-goo eyes they were making at each other (puke); what looked to be a father/daughter duo, but I guess you never really knew; a family—mom and dad eating and chatting as daughter ate cereal quite nicely and older brother tried to flip sugar packets into dad's coffee.

I decided to give it a rest before anyone noticed and focused back on my coffee. "Anything good?" Kathleen asked with a raised eyebrow. She seemed to be waking up some. I grinned sheepishly.

"That obvious?"

Just then Liam came back and set a plate in front of each of us. Oh yum. Just inhaling the wonderful aroma of bacon and potatoes was enough to wake me up further.

"I will be back with some fresh waffles, but this should start you for now." With a smile and a nod he turned to walk away, and we dug in.

We ate in silence for a while, only slightly pausing to look up when waffles were placed in front of us. I held it to just the one, but that was one of the best waffles I had ever tasted. Maybe something to do with the mountain air. We were just relaxing back with more coffee when Liam came rushing to the table.

"Girls, there is to be a big break in the weather. I would love to keep having you, but if you want to get anywhere else, now is the time."

Kathleen and I looked at each other in surprise. "Really?" I finally said. "We *were* kind of hoping to see more before landing at the wedding." Kathleen was nodding and looking out the window.

"Well, whenever you are ready, just gather your things and we will get you on the road."

Thirty minutes later we stood in the entryway, bags packed, bill paid, and feeling a little harried. More time in this little respite would have been nice, but seeing more and making our way towards the wedding was better. Louise had come out of the kitchen too, declaring folks had quite enough food for now and could wait a bit. I found I was going to miss her, even after only knowing her a short time.

"Well, girls, you will just have to come back and see us again. For right now, you have other adventures to attend to." Liam paused and looked at me as if trying to figure something out. "You started in Dublin, right?"

"Yes, we spent a few days there before coming here," I answered, trying to think why he would be asking.

"And where did you stay there, loves?" Louise jumped in. "I don't think Liam told me. We like to keep up on the competition you know," she finished mischievously.

"Baggot Court," I replied. "Beautiful place—we really enjoyed it."

"Not as much as here, though," Kathleen hastily threw in.

Our hosts exchanged a look, then Louise threw her head back and laughed. "Off with you then. You have a lot of road to cover to see our beautiful country."

"You'll be crossing the River Shannon, correct?" We nodded to Liam's question. "You might spend some time in the town of Tarbert, then. Lovely little town, just at the ferry stop. Can't miss it."

Louise seemed to be covering a smile, but it could have been my imagination. "Well, then," Liam finally said. "Have a lovely time, and I am sure we will be crossing paths again soon enough."

Saying another thank you for the wonderful time and food, Kathleen and I grabbed our bags and turned to walk out the front door. We wheeled our bags down the small steps and across the pebbled drive to the car.

The air had that damp freshness right after a rain, and the sun was brilliant—perfect to drive and see the landscape. This time, I hopped behind the wheel (which I had to remind myself was on the right side of the car) and prepared for my first international driving excursion. We figured quiet mountain roads would be the nicest place to start.

"What do you suppose Liam meant about seeing us again?" Kathleen asked from the passenger seat as I got situated.

"Oh, probably just being friendly. A good hospitable host and everything."

"Hmm." She seemed thoughtful. Probably fearing for her life as I got ready to take this on.

Thankfully, we had rented a car with automatic transmission, so I didn't have to worry about shifting gears. I eased the car onto the lane heading up the hill toward the main road, keeping a careful eye on the left side as I tried not to freak out too much with the edge of the road so close to me. No one was out and about yet, so I made it to the top with no resistance.

Kathleen studied the map and gave directions here and there from the passenger seat. Soon, we were out onto more open road and making our way towards Graiguenamanagh. I was excited to see what this town was about, especially since Anne had such good things to say about it. Speaking of ... I hadn't talked to her in a bit. Maybe I would give her a call when we arrived.

Kathleen popped the trip CD into the player and Willa Ford's "I Wanna Be Bad" came blaring out of the speakers. Uh-oh. Was this a sign of our evening to come? I smiled at the thought. Music, some good pub time. I couldn't wait. From the way Kathleen was rocking out next to me, it seemed she was in the spirit too.

An uncomfortably close brush with a lower hanging branch brought my concentration back to the driving. I was on an established two-lane, cement road, but it still felt pretty narrow at times. Navigating through towns and cities would be interesting, but for now I would enjoy getting used to the feel of the car. So far, so good. Kathleen's eyes started to close, which I took as a good testament to my skills. I tried to keep my driving as smooth as possible and watched for signs to our turnoff.

# 16

The town *did* feel a little magical. It could have been the joy of being out of the car finally, but I got such a good feeling walking the streets. We had parked next to a waterway with boats in various colors docked here and there and a narrow cobblestone bridge crossing it. Getting the lay of the land on foot seemed like a good idea, and we were starting to think of food and lodgings.

"I could use something to drink," Kathleen said, scanning the store fronts across the street. "And maybe we could get some local help again."

"Sure, sounds good. Where to?"

"How about right there," she replied, pointing across the street.

I nodded and we entered the pub behind another group of people. I paused and looked around. Kathleen did the same. The place was fairly full for this early in the day so it must be pretty good. There were a few empty tables close to us and another room to our right, but we decided to go to the bar first.

Kathleen ordered ciders for us (I was converting her), and I carried them to a table while she paid. I took a sip of mine to keep it from spilling and glanced over to see her still talking with the bartender. She nodded and slipped off her barstool, crossing to me with a triumphant smile on her face.

"I got us a room."

"What? Seriously?"

"Yeah, the bartender knows the owner of a place called the Waterside Inn—just around the corner. Said it's really nice."

"Hey, yeah ... sounds perfect."

"He also said they have great food and music here, and we should leave our car where it is and stay."

"Well, alrighty then. Another round and some burgers!" I had seen some go by, and they smelled too good to pass up.

"Now you're talking!" Kathleen's face lit up in the biggest smile I'd seen in the past couple of days. Good—we would stay here as long as we needed to. She took a sip of her cider and went back to the bar to order food.

It was approaching noon and more and more people were streaming into the pub; I wondered if they knew something we didn't. Maybe how great the food was. Two rather handsome gentlemen, maybe close to our age, also came in carrying various instruments. One guy set down the cases he was carrying in a front corner of the room and went back outside; the other took his armful through a door behind the bar and disappeared. Curious.

Kathleen joined me at the table again and looked around. "What's with all the people? I guess we picked the right place."

"I was just thinking the same thing. Sláinte to that!"

"Sláinte! And I'll do you one better—"

Timed perfectly, the bartender arrived and placed two shot glasses on the table. Kathleen winked at me and raised her glass. "Let's get this party started."

"Well, okay! *Now* we're talking ..."

I clinked my glass against hers and raised it to my lips. The Jameson went down nice and smooth. Great appetizer.

I cast another glance at my friend as she scanned the crowd, remembering what she'd said at Riversdale House. About life feeling stale and getting away from her. How could I help with that? Not that I was the expert on how to be thoroughly fulfilled, but I'd tried to take advantage of opportunities as they'd come my way. I'd have to keep my eyes out and see if I could guide her towards anything. Sometimes it helped having someone who knew you well nudge you towards something that could be good for you —I knew from experience. For now I'd nudge her towards booze and a good time.

"*Woohoo!* Music time!"

Amazing what two hours of cider and Jameson could do. Luckily the crowd at large had started the cry, and Kathleen was just joining in. She took a swig of her cider and toasted the girl next to her. It was nice seeing my friend really let loose. I took a swig of my own drink and realized I was feeling pretty good too. The burger and fries had been delicious, but maybe not quite enough.

I turned to Kathleen and felt the room sway a little. "Men suck. I don't know if I want one after all."

"So now we're talking about this." She slung an arm around my shoulder. "All right—let's hear it."

"How could he pull that crap? I mean really?!"

"Because men do suck. They suck indeed." She nodded quite solemnly, as if saying something of great wisdom.

"It was like driving a car, y'know? He just pulled the E-brake and slammed into reverse!" Now I was on a roll.

"Well, at least it landed you in the city with all the opportunities and excitement. My life is so boring." She looked so despondent I almost had to laugh.

"Oh, my friend," I replied and raised my pint glass. "On that note—" I took a swig and Kathleen laughed, following suit. "And what is with that Padraig guy?! I thought he was kind of interested and he was all stiff huggy when we left. Whatever." Now I was starting to feel a little depressed myself. "I think I'm drunk."

Kathleen laughed again and stood up. "I think he *does* like you, and you *are* drunk. Now, it's time to stop all this, because the band is starting to play and we must dance!"

I laughed in spite of myself and nodded, pushing my chair back to stand up. As I rose to stand next to her, I noticed Kathleen freeze, her face gone blank. Hmm? I turned to follow her gaze and wound up looking at the band.

"I think that's him," Kathleen said, sounding as if she were in a trance.

"Who?" I turned to look again and a fuzzy memory began to form as I eyed the guy who had just walked up to the mic. "Thing Mote guy? *Stairs guy*?" Oh, this was just getting too good.

I can honestly say I had not seen Kathleen that thrown and unsure of what to do. She just stood there frozen and staring, not even trying to play it off. Oh boy. Luckily no one else seemed to notice. Everyone was wrapped up in their own people and celebrations. No one paid attention to one tipsy American and her befuddled, probably instantly sober, friend.

I finally tapped her arm to bring her back. She looked at me, still a bit glazed, but then seemed to focus. I pulled her down into her chair and slid her pint glass across the table, thinking I'd just found my next nudge moment. She took a swig and shook her head a bit.

"Holy *crap*. It's him! Am ... what should I do?!"

"What should you do? Well, for starters you have to say hi—see if he remembers you. Wasn't he your best random, crazy story? Kind of the one that got away?"

"Yes. I mean, I kind of regretted not looking for his band after that night."

"Well then—"

"I'm sure he does *not* remember me. I'll be just another crazy band groupie throwing herself at the hot musician. No. *Way* too embarrassing."

"Well, what about if your drunken friend went up and made an embarrassing spectacle and you had to go and stop her? Or save the band from her inappropriate behavior."

"You wouldn't!"

"I don't know. I've had quite a bit of Jameson, and I'm in a feisty mood ..."

"All right, all right!"

"Let's just go up and dance. Others are starting, so it won't be weird. And if you just happen to get close to the front of the pack and make eye contact with the lead singer ..."

She smiled. "Yeah, okay. I guess that's not so bad. What can I say? You've learned a lot from Anne."

"Why, thank you." Anne was known for being pretty fearless and clever. She would be proud to know she had rubbed off on her more cautious sister, who was now trying to make something happen for her friend.

We grabbed our drinks and made our way towards the front of the room. The crowd really *was* on their feet and starting to dance, so our plan was a good one. I took the lead and angled well so we ended up at the front of the group but just off to the side. No need to be *too* obvious. I moved back slightly so Kathleen had the clearer view of him.

I seriously could not have imagined it going better than it did. Kathleen was definitely nervous but keeping it in well. She swayed to the music along with the rest of the crowd and scanned the band members in equal turn, so not too obvious. He was singing a line and scanning the crowd when he caught sight of her, and I swear I heard his voice catch. He continued to sing, but paused and kept his eyes on her, looking as if he were trying to place her. I too was trying to be casual and not act as if I were watching this scene with baited breath. Kathleen was in front of me and blocking my view for the most part, anyway.

The band played another song, and then the singer leaned in to talk to his bandmates. He turned back to the crowd and, glancing in turn at Kathleen and the crowd at large, announced that they were taking a short break and would be back soon. Dancers started dispersing and

Kathleen turned to me, not sure what to do. I was about to suggest we go back to the table to regroup when I saw someone tall approaching her from the side.

"Sorry," said a very deep voice, and Kathleen's eyes went wide. She turned as he continued. "You look very familiar. Have we met before?"

"Yes, actually," Kathleen managed to say. "It was a while back, but I saw one of your shows in Dublin. Thing Mote."

He thought for a moment and then smiled. "*That's* it. The stairs ..."

Oh boy. She *had* made quite an impression with that. I tried to keep the smile off my face at the memory. He seemed to notice me then.

"This is my friend, Amelia. She was there too. Oh, and my name is Kathleen." She seemed to be gathering her wits. "I don't think we exchanged names when we met before."

"My name is Cian." (That was Kathleen's favorite Irish name.)

"That's my favorite name!"

*Oh my, she said it.*

"I m-mean ... " she stammered.

"Well, I'm glad to have it then," Cian cut in with a wink.

Kathleen must have been dying. This was so great! The look on her face said it all. My friend looked so happy. This Cian guy looked pretty happy too. They talked for a bit longer—I really had no idea what about as I was trying to be nonchalant and give them their space. I scanned the room and made conversation with some girls next to me. Soon enough, though, the band was regathering and grabbed Cian to start their next set. He seemed hesitant to leave Kathleen, but took his place at the microphone.

We walked to the bar for more drinks, Kathleen with a nice dreamy look on her face. Since most people were back on their feet and dancing, we had no trouble getting space and ordering our pints. I even got us two more Jamesons to commemorate the occasion. All that dancing had sobered me up a bit.

"So?" I couldn't stand it any longer. She needed to spill.

"So …" Her smile and giggle said it all. The shock seemed to have worn off, and she was just glowing. She looked excited and relaxed at the same time, if that was possible. "Omigosh, Am, that was *perfect!* He's amazing and so nice. So mellow for someone obviously very popular. And those eyes."

Okay, now she was on a roll. As she gushed, the bartender came over with our drinks and told us they were courtesy of the band. He winked at Kathleen and walked away. Now I *knew* she was going to swoon. She turned to look at the band, and Cian was smiling over at her. She raised her glass to him with a smile of her own and turned back to me with the most radiant look on her face. Oh boy, she had it bad.

We headed to our little table and continued to watch the band from our seats. More people had abandoned the dance area, so we had a fairly clear view. Kathleen was happy to sit back and gaze at her lead singer, though she *did* try to be a little discreet. I noticed a few girls throwing looks her way as if wondering who this stranger was trying to move in on the handsome front man.

After a bit of time the band took another break, and the guys started disappearing through the side door by the bar, maybe a backstage area for performers. I saw Cian glance over at Kathleen (an invitation?) but then continue walking behind the others. Kathleen looked as if she wanted to follow, but seemed resigned to staying with me at the table.

Nudge time.

"Go on," I said, to put her out of her misery. "Go follow your singer. How many chances like this do we really get?"

"You're sure? I can't leave you alone sitting here. How rude is that."

"I will be just fine and actually much happier knowing you're grabbing life by the horns or balls or whatever it is."

She gave me a grateful smile. "Thanks, Am. You're the best. I won't be long!" And she too disappeared through the door.

I took another sip from my pint glass and let my gaze roam around the room. With the band gone quiet, just about everyone sat at tables, talking amongst themselves—tossing back shots and slamming their glasses down. A few people still stood about the room, as seats were all taken, and a few continued to dance. It sounded like a rousing game of darts was going on in the next room, though I could only catch glimpses of people and the dartboard.

My brain was still pleasantly fuzzy, even with all the excitement. And given the recent turn of events for my friend, I allowed myself to entertain thoughts of my own Irishman. While I was still skeptical (and feeling mature in being so), how fun would it be? After my pep talk to Kathleen, should I take my own advice? Somehow look Padraig up and try to get in touch with him from here; try and make something happen? What, I did not know. I supposed I could just wait until we returned to Dublin and gage it from there. Funny how my great new job at West Coast Press had been pushed to the back burner in so little time. Thoughts of looking more seriously into bed and breakfasts with Anne had been entering in too. Interesting.

After what seemed a brief amount of time, Kathleen returned to the table and the band climbed back on stage. My friend still appeared a little in shock—but very, very happy. She dropped into her chair and kind of looked at me, then seemed to snap out of it and leaned forward, grabbing my forearm. "You will *not* believe this. They're playing at Anne's wedding!"

I just stared at her. I'm sure the shock on my face matched hers, and all I could do was shake my head. It was definitely fun to see my normally calm and collected friend so thrown and excited. This wasn't a nudge, but a shove!

"What? *How?*" was all I managed before the band started playing again. Kathleen gave me a look that said she'd share more later, and we both returned our attention to the stage.

It was soon too loud to talk much, and Kathleen was focused solely on Cian. He seemed a bit distracted too. He kept locking eyes with Kathleen (much to the chagrin of the other females in the room), but still managed to perform a great set. These guys were *really* good.

My thoughts started to wander and I found myself envious of my friend, even as I felt a bit guilty for it. Basically Kathleen was guaranteed to see him again. She really did deserve this time to be on her own and exploring what *she* wanted to be about. And who she wanted to explore it all with. If only some magical turn of events would have Padraig show up too.

I forced myself back to the energy of the room and the big smile on my friend's face. She was still caught up in the music and fun, and I was *not* going to interrupt that.

We danced some more, finished our drinks, and then the band was finished and it was time to make our way to the hotel. Kathleen was still trying to play it cool, but there was also a genuine excitement between her and Cian, and he seemed to be a really nice guy. They shared some brief words, while I pretended not to listen, then he and the rest of the band waved good night to me, and we were out the door.

We linked arms as we walked down the street, as seemed to be our habit over here, and drank in the night air, which was nice after so long inside a small room with many bodies. I finally looked over at her with a "Yeah that just happened," and we burst into giggles.

The hotel was indeed only a short walk away and even close to where we had parked. We grabbed our bags and checked in quickly. The night of frivolity had taken its toll, even if in a good way, and sleep was quite welcome.

# 17

Kathleen's head was in the clouds, and I was not at all surprised. Good thing I was comfortable behind the wheel now and had a fairly straight shot, because I had totally lost my navigator.

The night before had been quite the thing. I had slept like a baby after our day and night of drink, song, and dance, but I was not so sure she had. How could she, with thoughts of that beautiful and talented man who had haunted her all this time swirling through her head. She had woken up refreshed enough, though, and even seemed a little more energized for the rest of our trip, especially the end. Hmm. I wondered why.

We were now heading towards the Ring of Kerry to see as much along the thirty-mile drive as we could on our way to the ferry crossing in Tarbert. We had both driven it before so knew what it held, and we wanted to get to Doolin to be part of the wedding setup. It was just too beautiful to pass up entirely.

I cranked up the volume on the radio and "Summer Wine" by the Corrs and Bono sounded through the speakers. Fitting. My head was not quite as clear as it could have been. A nice hearty breakfast in the pretty dining room on the bottom level of the hotel had helped, but I had still taken two ibuprofens.

Kathleen turned her head against the seat and looked at me. "Sorry I'm so quiet. I think I just spaced out for a full five minutes."

"Oh, that's fine." I laughed. "You've put up with the same from me. So—how you feeling? Come on, we need to be girls and freak out about this."

"Okay, *that* I can do. Sheesh, I mean—*seriously*? We were *just* talking about him and *poof*! Here he is! How does that *happen*?"

We giggled as she did air quotes to copy the line from *Say Anything*. "It happened because you deserve it, and it was meant to. The universe is speaking to you! Saying, 'Kathleen, it's your turn for amazing things so just accept them and be happy. And by the way, don't screw it up.'"

"Gee, thanks." She laughed. "No, no pressure at all."

"So, he and the band will be playing at the wedding. So you will absolutely see him again."

She nodded.

"And how did that come about, did he say? I mean, how did Anne and James connect with them? I don't think we even got their name that one time we saw them."

She nodded again. "Cian couldn't remember how it all got set up, but they do have another gig on the way to Doolin. Maybe just combining work when they're on this coast? Oh, and it seems like they'll be crossing the river at the same place we are. That town—Tarbert? Maybe we'll see them there too." The hopefulness in her voice was endearing.

"Yeah, you never know. Well I can't wait to talk to Anne and get more info. She will freak out." I glanced at Kathleen from the corner of my eye. "Are you happy I made you go talk to him?"

"*Yes,* okay? Are you happy now?"

"Quite, thank you very much." I gave her a self-satisfied smile. "And are you feeling any better about things in general?"

"Yeah, I guess." Suddenly she looked very far away. Hmm. So something was still going on there.

"Well, one piece of excitement at a time. Since you're not the worrywart like me, I won't drag you down. Maybe you'll rub off on me. Give me some of your juju."

She just smiled and looked forward. Just like that, I had lost her again. That was fine. I would leave her to her thoughts. Listen to the music, take in the scenery as we wound our way across to the west side of the island, and try and let my own thoughts rest for a while.

Willa Ford's "I Wanna Be Bad" was next up. How did that song keep coming back around? The universe was *definitely* trying to tell us something, I thought, and laughed to myself. Before I knew it we were seeing signs for the Ring of Kerry.

# 18

You have got to be kidding me. I looked over at Kathleen who was just as dumbfounded as me. How could the sign say: "TERMINAL CLOSED: NO FERRY SERVICE"?

We were standing at Shannon Ferry Limited near the town of Tarbert, ready to buy our tickets and cross the river to be on our way to the wedding. It was in four days, and we hoped to be in Doolin by this evening to join the festivities. Our trip through the Ring of Kerry had been wonderful, and now we were ready to be with friends and family.

"Let's ask that guy over there," Kathleen suggested, pointing to a man further down the dock.

We headed that way, now noticing how quiet this place was. You would think a main outpost on a busy waterway would be hopping. I felt a vibration in my pocket and realized my phone was ringing.

"It's Anne. She'll definitely be wondering where we are."

"Answer it, and I'll see if I can find out what's happening," Kathleen replied. She walked towards the man, and I hit the answer button on my phone.

"Hey! How are you—*where* are you?" I could hear the excitement in Anne's voice and was sorry not to be there.

"Well, I'm not sure," I replied, a bit hesitantly.

"What? You guys okay?"

"Oh, yeah, we're fine. We're at the ferry terminal, but it's closed and a sign says no boats are operating." I was sure my sister could hear the distress in my voice.

"Oh, shoot! I wonder with all this rain … sometimes the banks flood and they stop all river crossings for safety."

"*What*?"

"Oh no, I want you guys here!"

"I know. Me too! Kathleen's asking someone here. Hopefully he knows, and it's just a temporary thing?"

"Well, that would be good. I need my sister!"

I smiled, picturing Anne's face as she said it. Kathleen came rushing back to me. The look on her face was not good.

"He said the banks are flooded, and they've stopped all traffic!"

"Oh nooo," I moaned into the phone. "Anne, you were right."

"Did he say for how long?" I asked Kathleen.

She shook her head dejectedly. *Well, crap.*

"I want you guys safe more than anything." Anne's voice brought me back to the phone.

"Thanks. I guess we'll hang out and get something to eat—maybe find a place to stay for the night. I want to stay close, in case the ferry opens up."

We said our goodbyes, and I promised to keep her updated. I turned to Kathleen and threw up my hands. She had about the same reaction.

"Well, okay. So there is nothing we can do. What time is it—are you hungry?" Suddenly, I was totally flustered.

"It *is* lunchtime. I guess I could eat something."

We both scanned around for places to eat nearby. A bunch of quaint storefronts greeted us but nothing jumped out, so we decided to walk a bit. In not too much time we saw a place called the Shannon Bar—perfect. A drink was definitely in order.

We walked inside and headed straight for the counter, ordering our drinks as if our lives depended on it. The bartender gave us a bit of a glance and then turned to pour our pints. I gave him my card to keep the tab open (who knew how long we would be there), and we made ourselves comfortable.

I sat and stared over my glass, suddenly tired. Kathleen seemed to be doing the same. What a pair we must have made—brooding into our drinks in a pub in the early afternoon.

"Anything to eat, girls?"

I looked up at the bartender and shook my head with a smile. "You?" I turned to Kathleen. She shook her head too, and we thanked him with a "Maybe later." We returned to our drinks, and I could not help thinking about Padraig. And my relationships. And men in general.

Our night in Graiguenamanagh had really let loose some things I had been holding inside, in a good way. It was nice to have time and distance, so I could give attention to thoughts I had pushed away. It felt safer somehow—more detached.

Those first few months had been really rough and were actually more of a blur trying to think back on. I had come so far to get back to *me* and had built a bit of a wall around myself. It was just easier to compartmentalize and move on. Maybe my lesson here was not that I had found this amazing Irishman while on vacation, but that I was just opening up again. I guess that was good enough.

"Hey, you in there?" I turned to Kathleen with a rueful smile. "I'm tired of sulking."

"Yeah, me too. We're in Ireland—only fabulous thoughts!" We both laughed at that, knowing it was not quite so easy. Problems generally followed you wherever you went. "Well, you finally found some excitement. So, Cian, huh?"

There was that big smile again. Even if she was thoughtful, my friend was happy. Just remembering her face when she first saw him— as if she'd been hit by a truck and the sun was finally coming out at the same time. I really hoped my gut feeling was right, and he was there with her. He *seemed* genuine in his excitement to see her again at the wedding.

"I still can't believe it. I really can't," Kathleen said. "I mean, what are the odds? And the *wedding*. We really can't be stuck here for too long, or I'll flip out."

"Well, yes, me too," I said, with a laugh. "And so will Anne. She was trying to be nice on the phone, but I could tell she was stressed. We haven't even thrown her a bachelorette party yet. She'll need time to recover—"

"Oh right. I hadn't thought of that. Are any groomsmen there yet? Has James done his thing?"

"I think most people are there by now, but not sure about the bachelor party. I would call and ask Anne, but I don't want to remind her why we should be there." I let out a little sigh, and then did a mental head shake.

"Alright, enough of this," I continued. "Yes, we are off our plan and it sucks, but it happens. You never know what can happen on a road trip, which is why they are so much fun, *so* ..." I paused to take a breath. "I say we have some food because we haven't eaten in a while and need lunch; explore town a bit because I'm sure it's awesome; and check back in at the ferry terminal every so often."

Kathleen sat straight up and gave me a mock salute. "Ay, ay, captain!"

I nudged her arm and laughed, hoping I had not sounded too bossy. We scanned the menus the bartender had left for us and ordered carrot soup (I love the blended vegetable soups) and brown bread, our moods decidedly lifted.

We left the pub with a little more bounce in our step. The area seemed pretty quiet, so we figured nothing was happening at the ferry station yet and decided to explore. The bartender had said there was a visitor center and museum, Tarbert Bridewell. Why not take advantage of this unexpected stay and see another piece of the continent?

"Looks like Liam is getting his wish," I said to Kathleen to break the silence. "He seemed to really like this town, so I'm sure we will too." I smiled thinking of him and Louise, surprised to find I actually did miss them.

We saw someone coming our way along the sidewalk and, hoping he was local, decided to ask for further directions to the museum. As he got closer, he looked up and our eyes met. I froze. Kathleen burst out laughing.

# 19

Padraig's face must have matched mine. It was classic. I think both our brains shut down as we stared at each other, trying to grasp that we were actually seeing each other.

Next to me, Kathleen was saying something, "... so good to see you. We just got here—stuck actually ..." and I finally zeroed in on her.

Padraig finally smiled and seemed to regain himself. "Well, it is certainly nice to see you two. You must be towards the end of your tour then; on your way to the wedding. You're stuck, you say?" He looked quizzically at me.

"We came here to take the ferry over to Killimen and then up to Doolin. The ferries aren't running right now because of the weather and the water level, so yeah. We're stuck." A thought struck me. "Hey, we have a car! I didn't even think of this ... Can't we just drive along the river until the land connects again? Like in Limerick? It would be a bit of a backtrack, but not too far."

Padraig looked thoughtful and shook his head. "The roads could be closed too. You just never know."

"You seem to know a lot about the area," Kathleen interjected. "What brings you here, anyway?"

"I grew up here, actually. I had a weekend off and decided to visit my folks. It's been awhile and seemed a good time." Now he looked a bit embarrassed, but I could not figure why.

"Well, this world—this *island*—just keeps getting smaller and smaller. We can't shake you!" I said this with a smile and hoped it didn't come out too harsh. Padraig did seem a little taken aback, but answered with a smile of his own. "I'm glad we can't," I added hurriedly, to cover any awkwardness.

"Yes." Kathleen chimed in. "Now we have a *real* local to show us around. We figured while we had some time here, we should see some sights. Are we close to the museum and visitor center?"

"Bridewell? Oh sure, I can take you if you like."

"Are you sure?" I asked. "That would be great, but we wouldn't want to keep you from anything."

"Actually, I was just out for a walk. Clearing my head a bit—walking down memory lanc."

I was quickly losing interest in the museum and wondered what Padraig had been thinking of, what his childhood here had been like. I was even happy just to look at his face as he continued the conversation with Kathleen, but I didn't want to seem too obvious or silly. Maybe it wasn't only the idea of him—but *him*—that I really did like and was opening up to.

We fell into step together as Padraig guided us onwards and I tried to join the conversation here and there, but inside I was jumping up and down and clapping like a little schoolgirl. I seriously could not dream up something as cool as this. To meet this really nice and *cute* guy, then have him turn up in all these unexpected places. And I swore there was interest from his side too, from the little glances he kept throwing my way. Whatever I felt when we left Dublin, I must have imagined or misread. Amazing, too, that I had sworn to myself I would be smart with this and not overthink; yet here I was. I shook my head and chuckled at myself, then hoped no one had noticed.

I tuned back in to Padraig, as he pointed out spots he had visited as a child, and soon we were there. Tarbert Bridewell turned out to be a jail and courthouse, used until 1874 and the 1950s respectively. It was a neat building with rooms of models re-enacting various scenes. (We giggled at a few of them). Overall it was a neat place to see, and the teacher in Kathleen especially enjoyed the history. Padraig seemed fairly fascinated with it too, saying he had only been there once when it had opened as a museum back when he was in high school.

We decided to bypass the gift and coffee shops and return to the ferry terminal to check on the situation. Again, Padraig entertained us with stories from his past—which corner he had chased his brother around only to run smack into the local priest; which house he had first lived in (his parents and grandparents now lived further outside of town); the pub David and Cora had been caught trying to sneak into in high school. I found myself quite enthralled with all of this, seeing his spirit and the similarities with my own upbringing, and hoped I did not look too dopey.

As it happened, Kathleen did most of the talking and asked questions about various places we passed. She glanced at me every so often, so I think it was deliberate, and I was grateful. I was sure she knew my brain was spinning.

We came to the terminal only to see that things were still closed down. There were workers scattered about doing various maintenance and monitoring the situation, but none could give us any sort of estimate on when we might be able to cross. One gentleman even suggested finding a place to stay for the night before things sold out with others facing the same situation. Oh boy.

Kathleen and I looked at each other a moment, knowing this had been a possibility, but not quite ready to face it. We had passed some buildings that looked like hotels or B&Bs, but I hadn't really been paying attention, especially after we ran into Padraig.

Padraig cleared his throat, seeming a bit nervous. "I don't mean to step out of bounds, but I'm staying at a nice place not too far from here that should have rooms available. At least it was quiet this morning."

"No, that's great," I rushed to assure him. "Thank you for the help.

We really are out of our element here."

"Well then. Let's get you there before you are in a foot race for the last room," he replied.

This made me think of one of my favorite shows, *The Amazing Race*, and I laughed as we started towards the B&B. In no time at all we stood in front of a charming yellow building called Keldun House. A woman came to the door and smiled at Padraig, then saw Kathleen and me and waved us in.

"What are you doin' standin' there, Padraig? Bring the girls in. Come on, come on." She laughed and backed up, holding the door open for us.

The first thing I saw as I walked in was—Cian. Oh boy, this was getting better and better. Then Kathleen saw him, and I thought she was going to faint. She'd gotten her wish—and maybe didn't quite know how to handle it. He turned and saw her, and his face broke into a big grin. His bandmates were taking bags through a door, but Cian paused and waited for us. It was my turn to take over for a bit.

"Cian—hello! What are you guys doing here? Kathleen mentioned you might be coming through this way, but you had a gig, right?"

"Yeah," he said, glancing over at Kathleen. "It was cancelled, so we were going to take the ferry across and get a head start for the wedding. Have a little extra time in Doolin. I guess you guys are stuck too, and that's why *you're* here?"

"Yes, but it hasn't been so bad," I replied, glancing at Padraig and then quickly looking away. "This is a beautiful town and an added benefit to the trip. Padraig grew up here and has been showing us around." I said this as a way of introduction.

Padraig and Cian shook hands, and we stood there in awkward silence. I looked at Kathleen, again thinking she must be dying inside, and waited to see if she had composed herself yet. She still looked a bit stunned but managed a smile at Cian, and there was definitely joy in it.

"So, I guess you're all here as long as we are?" Kathleen asked. "Maybe we could see some of the town together. That is, unless you'll be practicing or spending time with the band." She tripped over her words at the finish.

Cian did not seem to mind though. He took her hand and raised it between them, pressing a light kiss onto the back of it. "It would be my honor, Kathleen," he said, with a wink, and released her hand. I think *I* died a bit; I could only imagine how Kathleen felt.

I heard a small giggle next to me. Yup, it got her. I looked at Padraig, and he was looking right back. We seemed to have the same thought: *These two should be alone.* Amazingly, with that my shyness and apprehension went away, and I felt a new bond with him. *Thanks, Kathleen!*

I shared my thoughts, and they agreed wholeheartedly. Cian was all too happy to really acquaint her with his band, and Kathleen was looking like she had just won the lottery. We made plans to meet in a couple hours for dinner back at the B&B, and I sent them off, figuring I would check us in.

The last thing I saw before they disappeared down the hall was Cian taking Kathleen's hand and her looking up at him with the most delighted smile on her face. I couldn't have been happier for my friend. It was fast, yes, but she deserved it.

I realized Padraig was talking to the owner and turned to join the conversation. I had forgotten she was there. I mentally shook my head. What a crazy trip this was turning out to be.

We resumed the introductions (it turned out Padraig knew the owner from childhood and was staying there to get some pointers), and I booked a room for Kathleen and me, which just happened to be next door to Padraig's (!!). When the details were settled, we lugged the bags to our rooms—and paused to look at each other. A bit of the shyness had returned, but I mostly felt a new camaraderie (and excitement still!).

"Would you like to get out of here? See a bit more of the town?" Padraig asked, looking so adorable I couldn't stand it.

"That would be nice. Yes."

He went to his room to grab a jacket, and I called Anne quickly to let her know where we were staying and give her the phone number as we generally did. Normally I would have filled her in on every detail, but I was so excited and anxious. Also, I got her voicemail so was a bit off the hook. I grabbed my own coat and, when I found Padraig, we headed down the road, in which direction I had no idea. I was still having a hard time getting my bearings.

"You've already seen one of our tourist attractions, so let me take you to a favorite place of mine now," Padraig said as we walked.

"Sounds great. I would love to see more of a local spot."

We ended up walking out along the water, which I must say I loved. I had always been drawn to water and spent lots of time at the beach back at home. I shared this with Padraig, and he smiled. Another commonality.

We walked and talked for I don't remember how long, sharing bits of this and that—Anne and I growing up in school together with different groups of friends; he and his brother growing up inseparable, but now not seeing each other so much; his parents being a solid example for him of a long and steady relationship; mine being divorced, but okay overall. At one point he reached over and took my hand (*Omigod— omigod— omigod*). His hand felt warm and strong, and it had been so long since I'd had that.

That was it. It felt more of a comfortable gesture as we continued to talk and share different stories and secrets. I was actually more excited by that, though, than any other action. The comfort and kinship of it felt more intimate somehow and was definitely something I had been wanting for some time now.

My thoughts switched to Kathleen and Cian and the craziness and excitement of that situation. I shared this with Padraig, and he was interested to hear the story from then and now. Even if he had only been our hotel manager for two days, he still seemed to feel protective of us, or at least cared for our well-being. He agreed that it was quite unbelievable, but also that perhaps the universe was coming around to play a hand for Kathleen. I loved that he had a bit of the superstition like I did.

A wind picked up. I commented that the water didn't seem all that treacherous, but Padraig assured me the surface could be deceptive. So we decided to turn back and seek a warmer place. He suggested Shannon Bar and I had to laugh, saying it had been our respite not too long ago.

"Well then, we both have good taste," he replied, and reached out to tickle me.

I was so surprised (he was being playful—flirty even!) and ran down the beach, shrieking and giggling as he chased after me. Oh, had I needed this. I could only imagine how pink my cheeks were going to be. When we arrived at the pub, he released my hand to open the door for me. Such a gentleman, but I will admit I was a bit disappointed—until I felt his hand on my lower back, gently leading me inside. I almost let out a sigh and batted my eyelashes at him.

Instead, I simply walked in and let him guide me to a small table against the wall. There were some larger groups in here (no doubt also waiting on the ferry system), which would make for some good people watching. Padraig rushed behind me as I started to take a seat, and I turned in confusion only to see him pulling out my chair for me. Boy, was he good.

I smiled as a thank you, but he had already rushed off towards the bar. Hmm. He came back rather quickly with a pint glass in each hand. We toasted, and I took a sip. Bulmers! A girl could get used to this. I thanked him and commented on how fast he had been served for the size of the crowd. He told me that the bartender had been his high school lab partner. Of course.

"So—" he began. "Back to Kathleen and Cian. Do you think they have a chance? I mean, a real chance?"

I loved that we were talking like old-time confidantes and partners though we had yet to establish any recognized bond between us. Still, I answered.

"It may sound crazy, but I think so," I replied. "From being with her on this trip and conversations we've had, I think she's ready for a big change. I mean, a drastic one. She's been very carefree and searching almost."

"Well, this would qualify as big," Padraig said, with a chuckle. "Cian seems a good guy. Nothing in the papers about him carousing about the country or tawdry behavior at his gigs."

I almost had to laugh at how serious he seemed about this and how fatherly he sounded. It was nice too, feeling like I had someone on my side to talk about things with. It had been a while since I'd had that. Of course I had my family and Kathleen, but this was different.

We made small talk for a bit—favorite sports and teams (football: 49ers, soccer/football: Manchester United), movies (*The Goonies, The Goonies!*), music (Josh Groban, U2). After a while, the conversation lapsed, and then Padraig took a deep breath.

"Remember what we were talking about on the beach? About Kathleen and Cian and the idea of fate?"

"Yes," I replied, wondering where he was going with this.

"Do you think that could be happening with us, too?"

*There's an us?*

"There's an us?" *Did I really say that out loud?*

He laughed a little self-consciously and looked down at the table, his beer clutched in his hands. "Well ... I would like to think so."

"Really?" I was sure I had the stupidest grin on my face. "Well, then ... Yes, I would like to think so too." I glanced down and could feel my face flushing bright red. I raised my eyes to find Padraig studying me intently, then he too looked away with a slight grin on his face.

How did people *do* this? No matter how old you were, the beginning stages of dating were so awkward. Admitting you *liked* someone. Well, it certainly was a scary ledge to step off, but so much fun too.

"I have to admit—I was thinking about you when I first saw you on the sidewalk. I was distracted—flustered. It was actually pretty embarrassing."

"Well, I can't say I reacted the best either," I admitted, to help him feel better. "So," I continued. "Where do we go from here then? You're here; I'm in California ..." "Where there's a will there's a way?" He laughed at the trite expression.

We fell silent for a bit, thinking, and the noise in the pub died down enough that we could hear the overhead music. The sounds of Coldplay's "Til Kingdom Come" filled the room, specifically the line about waiting. Okay, now that was just weird. Padraig must have thought so too, because he laughed a little and grabbed my hand, giving it a small squeeze.

"Maybe it's a bit early to be worrying too much. Let's just enjoy it and see where we go."

I nodded gratefully, readily agreeing with him. "That sounds good."

He excused himself to use the toilet and I sat back, listening to the song (one of my favorites). Wow—what had just happened? I grinned to myself, looking around but not really caring if anyone noticed. Could this really have just dropped into my lap? Maybe Kathleen was right and anything *could* happen—why not? And what did I really want out of all this? A relationship? Just a hot, sweaty fling? What did *Padraig* want? Certainly the looks we kept exchanging held heat and promise.

Well, this certainly was turning into one hell of a trip. I would have to thank Anne later. *Anne!* I hadn't even mentioned Padraig to her (or Cian. Oh, she was going to die), and she must have been wondering what was happening with us. Hmm—I should call her, but after Padraig came back, so he didn't think I'd run away after our conversation.

When Padraig returned we noticed the time (it flies when you're on cloud nine!) and realized that we needed to get back to the B&B to meet Kathleen. We gave up our table and walked hand in hand the short way to Keldun House.

Inside, we passed what was probably the dining room and saw Kathleen and Cian sitting at a table, looking to be deep in conversation. The first thing I noticed was that they were holding hands, and the second was that Kathleen looked very happy. I smiled for my friend and again thought what a hell of a trip this had been.

She looked up then and noticed us.

"Hi, guys!"

"Hi, yourself," I replied, as I walked into the room. Padraig followed me, and we pulled up chairs at their table. "Where's the rest of the band?"

"Oh, they left us a while ago," Cian answered. "Said they needed a drink and wanted to meet some ladies."

"So, what have you guys been up to?" I tried to ask as innocently as possible.

"Oh, just making up for lost time," Kathleen replied happily. "A lot has happened to both of us since we last saw each other."

Well, well. This seemed very serious indeed. They sure hadn't wasted any time.

"And how was your afternoon?" Cian asked us.

"Great! Padraig took me to a beach he knows, and then we went back to the pub we were at earlier to warm up a bit."

"I'll bet you did," Cian said, with a wink.

"Hey! I'm not that kind of girl. " But I couldn't help laughing—and thinking I kind of wanted to be. Where was this sauciness coming from?

"We had lots of witnesses. The place was packed! I guess lots of people got stuck waiting on the ferries."

"So, what time does dinner start anyway?" Kathleen asked.

"Ah!" Padraig stood up, startling us all. "Seven o'clock, and that is my cue. Thank you for the reminder. I said I'd help Mary with the prep and gain some valuable knowledge in the process." He said this with mock seriousness, gave me a parting glance, and was gone.

"So ..." Oh, this was awkward. I so wanted to talk to Kathleen alone and see what had gone on. There were stories to tell. "Are you going to stay here until dinner starts?" This was aimed at Kathleen, but I didn't want to be obvious, so I addressed Cian as well. "I was thinking of going back to the room for a bit—to rest, unpack ... " Kathleen finally picked up on it.

"Actually, I could do the same. Is that alright with you?" she asked Cian. "See you back here in a bit?"

The look they exchanged was almost too much to take. I averted my glance and stood up, taking my time gathering my things to give them a moment. They exchanged a brief kiss (*what?!*), and Kathleen preceded me out of the room. I gave Cian a small wave and hurried after her.

# 20

When I walked into the room, Kathleen was sitting on her bed, grinning at me like a looney bin. I could just feel the excitement coming off her. As I closed the door behind me, she bounced up off her bed and grabbed me in a big hug.

"Oh ... my ... *gawd* ..." she said, and started dancing around me. "I am going to stop being surprised by it now because this seems to be the trip of crazy things, but *really*?" She hugged herself, and I smiled at our little girly scene. "He *likes* me, Am! It's been a few years, but he said he's thought about me!" She put her hand over her heart, gave a girly sigh, and fell back onto the bed.

"Well, this trip certainly could not get any better, and we haven't even reached the wedding yet. We should have left the country sooner," I said with a laugh.

"We've had some interesting talks, Am." She seemed to be calming down and actually turned a bit serious. "Remember when I said I'd think on things later? Well it's later ... After *our* talk, I have really been thinking about what I can change and how badly I need it. Well, Cian's band is doing really well ..." She paused and took a deep breath. "Oh, man— you're gonna think I'm nuts. I can't really believe I'm saying this myself."

She paused again and shook her head to herself, embarrassed almost. What in the world was going on? Though, maybe I was starting to guess.

"The band needs a manager of sorts," Kathleen continued, "and quickly. They've looked all over, interviewed people, and nothing is working out. So—they've asked me. And it sounds really great, and is similar to work I've done before."

I think I was just staring at her in shock. The words were pouring out of her now. I remembered all the on-campus concerts she'd worked with during our college years, and how much she'd enjoyed it.

"And I think I'm in love with Cian. We haven't said anything about it yet 'cause that's crazy, but still. And our numbers at school are going down and since the beginning of the year there's been talk of eliminating a classroom, so I could volunteer with no problem and would actually be doing others a favor."

It seemed like she was almost asking permission or at least seeking approval from me. I was not quite sure what to say yet, so I walked over to her and gave her a hug. She seemed really happy about it and there was a new spark in her, so I was happy for *that*.

"I didn't tell you this earlier because I just wanted us to have a nice, fun trip but before I left, my principal and I talked about someone leaving by Thanksgiving—the budget is that much in trouble—so this wouldn't be that big a shock to them."

I finally found my voice. Shoot, we only lived once, right?

"Well, holy cow, what a day you've had! So, you want to stay then? After the wedding?"

She bit her bottom lip and nodded her head slowly. There was no hesitation or nervousness though, just excitement.

"Well, what can I say really? I guess I want to say slow it down a little and think on it some more, but I can't. This is exciting, and you deserve it! And it isn't like you're moving to some foreign place for someone else. Dublin was your home first, and you *have* missed it."

I gave her another hug and squealed a bit, giving her a squeeze and making her do the same.

"Crap, dude. I mean—*really*?! We wanted change—we got it!" I laughed. "Anne is going to *freak out*. Well, and be sad she missed it. Me and Padraig, you and Cian, you *staying*. "

Kathleen waved her hand and stared at me. "Wait a second. So there is a you and Padraig?"

I nodded and felt my face flush, remembering the things we had talked about, and she let out a *woohoo* that seemed to echo off the walls. We both stilled, wondering if anyone had heard us, and then the giggles set in.

"I feel like such a teenager. I love it. He held my hand as we walked by the water, which is so normal but I was just so ... *giddy* inside. I hope I didn't freak him out."

"Well, from the way he looked when you two came in, I would say not," she said with a glint in her eyes. "I *so* had a feeling, Am. I could just tell he was interested in you. Admit it. I was right."

"Okay, yes—you were right."

Her smile was self-satisfied. She loved being right. Who didn't, really? Then she glanced at her watch and said, "Oh wow! We'd better get to dinner. It's a little after seven."

We changed into nicer pants and tops (the reason we had come to the room) and hurried back to the dining room. Cian was there with his bandmates, who had decided to return from wherever they had been entertaining themselves, and stood when he saw us approaching. He held a chair out for Kathleen, and I took the one next to her. They had pushed two tables together to fit us all, so I was sure this would be a rousing evening. Tablecloths and plates and silverware had been placed on the tables, transforming the room from daytime to nighttime.

One of the guys (the drummer ... I think his name was Gerry) was telling a story when Padraig popped his head around the door and motioned to me. Curious, I excused myself and got up to see what he wanted.

As I walked through the door into the hallway, he grabbed my hand and pulled me towards the kitchen. Now my interest was really piqued, and I was sure he saw it on my face.

"I just thought you might want to see the food preparation, in case you really do decide to get into the B&B business like you were talking about," he said. His smile told me there might be other reasons too.

In the kitchen, Mary bustled around the small room to check different foods as they cooked. Trays of bread, and what looked to be cookies and rolls cooling, covered the counters. She kept stirring and checking various pots on the burners, and delicious smells came from two different ovens. What a production!

She looked up then and noticed us, waving us into her space. "Ah, here is your lady! Come in, come in. I could use another pair of hands."

His lady? Hmm—I kind of liked the sound of that. Padraig seemed a bit embarrassed, but there was no time to address this as Mary started giving us orders. Everything was to come out simultaneously and be fresh and piping hot for each guest. Padraig moved about the space with a deft efficiency (I hadn't thought about the cooking aspect of running a B&B) and seemed right at home.

Mary had me check on the rolls sitting on the counter as well as those still rising in the oven. At one point she leaned in close and said quietly, "He has talked of you often, you know," and then walked away. Wait, what? No, I need to hear more! Every so often she would give me knowing looks, but she kept busy preparing the meal for her guests.

When she gave the word, I started delivering baskets of bread and rolls as Padraig scooped soup into bowls to be carried out. Kathleen did a double-take when she saw me walk into the room with the baskets, but then went back to her conversation. I dropped off a basket at our table, smiled when she looked up questioningly, and returned to the kitchen for the next round. Padraig came in with bowls of soup on a tray, and he bumped my hip with his as we passed. He kept walking with an innocent smile on his face, and I giggled as I continued on to the kitchen.

Mary was dishing steamed vegetables into large serving bowls and handed me a tray for them. I waited as she worked, thinking about all the effort to produce this one meal. I would have to share this with Anne and get her take on it.

"He really is a special one, you know," Mary said, as she handed me a bowl. "Known him all his life, and you will not find a better kind." She handed me another bowl and smiled. "You seem to be made of good stuff too." Just like that—the stamp of approval. I had known this woman only a few hours, but I would take it. She said no more on the matter, and we continued working with our own little rhythm.

I was carrying the tray of vegetables through the kitchen doors when Padraig returned. As we passed, he gave me a smile that warmed me all the way to my toes. I really liked this guy. Spending time with him, doing whatever—even serving dinner to a room full of guests. Definitely not just a hot, sweaty fling. This could get complicated, but I really didn't care at the moment.

In the dining room, I went to our table first. "Your vegetables, madame?" I said as I put the bowl in front of Kathleen. She looked up with a *What is going on?* look on her face, and a few other guests glanced over. I decided to quit messing around, served the rest of the tables, and headed back for the kitchen.

As I was entering the kitchen, I ran into Padraig coming out. He took the tray out of my hands and put it on a counter, then turned me around and indicated we could go sit down. Mary yelled "Thank you!" from across the room, and we made our way back to the dining room.

He pulled my chair out for me (I could *definitely* get used to this) and then joined the table himself. This time Kathleen was openly staring so I finally said, "Padraig thought I might like to get a behind-the-scenes look at what goes into running a B&B."

"Oh, well that's nice. Makes sense," Kathleen replied. "Did you?"

"Yes, that a lot of work goes into just that one part," I replied, with a laugh. "Still, it was nice he thought of me." I said this quietly so that just Kathleen could hear (Padraig had joined into conversation with the guys, so I was relatively safe.) She nodded her understanding and patted my knee.

I gave a slight nod towards Cian in a silent *And how is that going?* She smiled and nodded a *Quite well, thank you.* I loved the silent conversations we could have.

Just then the lady herself came through the door with the main course. Mary placed a giant tray on a side table, then turned with a bowl in each hand and served the two nearest tables. She repeated this until each table had its own. We passed ours around (I liked this family-style dining), and when it came to me, I scooped what looked to be a chicken/potato/bread mix onto my plate. It smelled delicious.

I passed the bowl on to Padraig. Our fingers touched for a brief moment, and I felt a little tingle (I could get used to that too). Oh boy, where was my head going? He gave me a little wink and scooped some food onto his plate. This just felt so *domestic.* I wondered if Kathleen was having any of these same thoughts. Maybe I would ask her later.

After that, dinner was rather uneventful. We all must have been hungry, because we dug into our food and not a word was said for quite some time. There were occasional shared glances from all around the table, but overall everyone seemed happy to be eating delicious food and settling in for the night. It was actually nice to feel so mellow and comfortable.

Cian's bandmates (I *had* to learn their names) excused themselves first, then Cian and Kathleen followed close behind. I was happy to sit with Padraig and observe the room. I even helped Mary clean up a bit. Finally, the last guests wandered out and Padraig and I followed, deciding to call it a night.

We walked slowly down the hall in the same direction (I had almost forgotten his room was right next door to ours) and paused in front of my door. I didn't hear any sound coming from the other side of the door so figured Kathleen was already in bed or at least getting close.

As I turned to say good night, Padraig leaned down and pressed his lips to mine. It was the lightest of touches and fairly brief, but I felt my whole body tingle. He straightened again, said good night with a small smile, and disappeared through his own door.

I stood there staring for I didn't know how long, then opened my door and entered the room. Kathleen was in bed, but she was not asleep. She was actually staring at me quite expectantly.

"I heard you guys walking down the hall. Where have you been?"

Then, she studied my face more closely.

"He kissed you, didn't he! Oh, tell me everything."

She was out of bed now and jumping around me. All I could do was feel dazed and very, very happy. I finally looked at her and then started to giggle. I was being such a *girl* but couldn't help it, and Kathleen understood. Hell, she'd started it! I tried to shush us before we got too loud (Padraig was *right* next door), told her it was amazing, and that we should go to bed. I wanted to share with my friend but also wanted to revel in the moment a bit.

Kathleen crossed the room and got back into her bed, grumbling. She gave me a quick smile, though, so I knew she understood.

"Good night, sleep tight, yadda yadda ..." I heard muffled from across the room.

I laid down in my own bed with my thoughts racing a mile a minute. Really, I was visualizing myself running through a sun-filled meadow, jumping and leaping for joy with flowers raining down on my head. Had that *really* just happened? I was going to hope it had and look forward to what would come in the morning. I hoped it would not be too weird and uncomfortable, with our guards being down in a darkened empty hallway versus lots of witnesses and the glaring light of day. I couldn't wait to see what I dreamed about ...

# 21

I heard rustling right next to my head and cracked an eye open.
Another eye looked back, just a few inches from my face.

"Sorry," Kathleen said in a hushed whisper. "I was trying not to wake you."

"What time is it?" I mumbled, as I stretched. "You going somewhere?"

"Cian and I are going for a walk," she replied. "He said he wants to show me something."

I raised an eyebrow at her. I bet he did.

"Oh come on!" She burst out laughing. "Some place he went before, as a kid or something."

"Fine—whatever. You're a big girl. Did you have any breakfast?"

"I thought you said I was a big girl. *Yes,* I had some breakfast. Oatmeal and some juice. It's out in the dining room. You should get some."

I checked the clock by the bed—6:30 am! Good grief, no wonder I was having trouble shaking the cobwebs out of my brain.

"Why so early?" I finally asked.

She just looked at me, then continued rummaging through her pile on the floor. I could tell Kathleen was all giddiness and nerves, so I wished her a good time and shooed her out the door. Cian was waiting outside, looking rather excited too. As I closed the door and wandered towards my bed, I realized I had never asked what it was she was looking for. Huh. Wonder what it was.

I crawled into bed and stretched out flat on my back, determined to lounge a bit longer before getting up and starting the day. I had just drifted off when there was a light knock on the door. Well. I guess my day was starting after all. Still half asleep, I slowly opened the door.

There stood Padraig, looking a bit uncertain and altogether too cute for words. I stared a moment and then remembered I was still in my pajamas. Oh well, at least I was in decently nice sweats and tank top and the hair wasn't looking *too* crazed. When you knock on someone's door at 6:30 in the morning, you're gonna get what you're gonna get.

"Amelia," he said. "Good morning." He gave me a tentative smile. "I just wanted to see if maybe you were hungry. I was on my way to the dining room ..." He was so nervous it was cute.

"Actually, I am." I really was. All this early morning activity had my body thinking it was time to wake up and start the day. So be it. "Let me put on better clothes and I'll meet you down there in five minutes?"

He nodded and walked off down the hall. I closed the door and turned towards my bed, willing my brain to catch up. Clothes. Clothes would be good. I rummaged through my suitcase and found jeans, T-shirt, and shoes. I got dressed quickly, brushed my teeth (morning breath was *so* not sexy), swiped some mascara across my lashes (no need to look too I-just-rolled-out-of-bed), and headed for the dining room.

Padraig was sitting with a beautiful girl, maybe a bit younger than us, and I felt a stab of jealousy. Whoa girl, hold on now. Too soon for that! He turned then and saw me. A big smile crossed his face and he stood to greet me, giving me a kiss on the cheek (yeah!). The girl looked at me, too, and gave me a polite smile.

"And who is this, Padraig?" she asked.

Excuse me? There was a sense of familiarity there, ownership even, but I couldn't quite put my finger on it. I'm sure I just stood there awkwardly as we both waited for his response.

"Gwynn, this is Amelia," he said. "Amelia, this is Mary's daughter,

Gwynn. I've grown up watching over her as she ran about this town—and the B&B for that matter."

Okay, so that answered a bit and he had more of a big brother tone as he spoke. I still could not put my finger on her though. There seemed to be something different there, but she held out her hand and shook mine.

"Nice to meet you, Amelia. I hope you're enjoying your stay here. Someday, I hope to run the B&B, so I'm trying to learn as much from Mom as I can."

"Oh, great," I said. "Wow, there seems to be a lot of interest in that area lately. Padraig was just saying the same last night."

Gwynn looked at him with a smile, and there was a certain affection—but a heat too. *Ah-ha*, so that was it. Had she imagined them running this place together or something? Or was *my* imagination running away with me? Hmm. Maybe this all was very innocent. I would have to put Kathleen on the case.

I realized all was quiet and both Padraig and Gwynn were looking at me. I felt my face flush. Oh boy, how red was I going to get? "I'm sorry... what?" was all I could say. Had that really just happened?

"I'm sorry. It's early, and I woke you up." Padraig came to my rescue. "We'll let you get settled and drink some coffee before we start grilling you. I'll be right back."

I sat down and exchanged glances with Gwynn. She smiled, and it seemed open and genuine. I decided to give her the benefit of the doubt. Maybe I was just annoyed because Padraig and I had shared a moment last night and now things *were* a bit different. I had to share him for the time being.

"So, it must be fun having this place as a family business," I said to her. "Have you always wanted to run it? Do you work here now?"

She laughed, a light tinkling sound (sometimes I thought I sounded like a moose). She also tossed her blonde, nicely-curled hair over her shoulder (my curly, brown hair was feeling more and more frazzled by the minute). "I've always enjoyed the idea of hotels and bed and breakfasts and wanted my own since I was young, but I don't work here. That could be a bit too close to the family. I work at a place across town as the manager, though I frequently ask Mom for tips. It would be nice to keep this place in the family though, and I think Mom is ready to retire soon. She's put her work in, that's for sure."

"Well, it certainly is nice having a connection to a beautiful place like this." I wasn't sure what else to say so smiled at her and sat back in my chair. She gave me a warm smile in return and any hostility I thought I had sensed was gone. Maybe she was just an old friend and a bit possessive of her friend's happiness.

A steaming mug of coffee appeared before me and Padraig took the seat next to mine. He held my gaze for a moment, and I was all too happy to keep the connection. I may have even leaned towards him a bit. From the corner of my eye, I thought I saw Gwynn look away. Padraig held my gaze for a moment longer and even I could tell this would be awkward for a third person. Gwynn pushed her chair back and excused herself, saying something about getting along to her inn and guests. We both wished her a good morning. She nodded at each of us, holding her gaze on Padraig for a beat longer, then turned and disappeared through the dining room door.

When Padraig turned back to me, his expression made my heart flutter—and melt—at the same time (was that even possible?). So maybe nothing had changed in the last few hours.

"Did you sleep well?" he asked, as he watched me pour milk in my coffee and take a sip.

"I did, actually. You?" *Were we really having this inane conversation?*

"Better than I have in months."

Well, now things were getting interesting. He looked thoughtful, but didn't say anything for a moment. Finally, he asked, "Can I show you something? Can we go somewhere?"

I tried not to smile. I could just imagine what Kathleen would say.

"Sure. What did you have in mind, or is it a surprise?"

"It's a surprise."

"Can we eat some breakfast first? I'm starving."

"Oh, yes, sorry!" His face was hilarious, so stricken and apologetic. "I actually ate a bit ago and had come back for more coffee. I forgot you still needed food."

So, an *early* riser. I tucked that away to remember in the future. Great. Hopefully he was not an early morning exerciser too.

He jumped up and hurried over to the side table to get me a bowl of the infamous oatmeal. Such service! I took another sip of coffee, watching as he carefully made his way back to the table balancing the oatmeal and some toppings. His jeans fit him quite nicely, and his red T-shirt was striking next to his coloring. He set the bowls down, and my stomach growled at the delicious smells.

"You *were* hungry," Padraig said, with a laugh.

Okay, that was embarrassing. I grinned and started adding toppings to my oatmeal. Brown sugar, walnuts, milk—yum!

I ate rather quickly, noticing how close Padraig's leg was to mine (*sigh*), and soon we were headed out the door to start the day's adventure. He took my hand in his (so natural!), and we started walking through the streets of the town. It was quiet, but the stillness was beautiful. It was just after seven and the town was still waking up. I could see how people became "morning people." It really was a nice and gentle way to start the day, hearing only your own thoughts.

"You don't mind walking a bit, do you?"

*Define a bit.* "No, not at all," I said out loud. Walking like this with him felt so comfortable and exciting that I could do it forever. Well, that was a strong word, but still.

"Okay, good." There was that smile again. "I just wanted to show you more of my places around here. I saw Kathleen and Cian leaving and figured I would not be interrupting any plans."

"Oh, no, not at all. I'm all yours." Umm. I hope he hadn't taken that the way it sounded. I could feel a flush move up my neck, but he seemed not to notice. Hopefully I could just chalk it up to the cool morning air.

I was glad he had suggested grabbing a coat for our adventure. I huddled down into my fleece jacket, happy for its warmth.

We had walked maybe fifteen minutes or so and were leaving the paved streets, heading more towards open fields and graveled paths. I could hear more birdsong and rustling in trees and bushes. Where *were* we going exactly?

"So, this is where I used to spend a lot of time as a boy." It was almost as if he had heard me. "When we first moved out here from town, it was hard for me. Not having friends and stores right outside my door. Unfortunately, I can't say I adjusted all that well or quickly, but coming out here—it helped, and eventually calmed me down."

I could not picture Padraig being anything but a calm, well-mannered child.

"So, what kinds of things did you do?" I asked, wondering if that would be too personal to share with me, having known me only a short time.

"Oh, nothing too crazy I suppose. I just had a bad attitude with my family—talking back to my parents, staying out past curfew with my friends in town. That sort of thing."

"Wow. I can*not* picture that." I suppose I could imagine a bad attitude over something more serious, like fighting or stealing, but still. He was such a gentleman!

He smiled. "Well, I am glad I got over it and turned into the fine man you see before you." He gave a mock bow, and I couldn't help but giggle. "I have to say, Amelia. I love that laugh of yours. I have since we met, oh—a week ago? Boy."

We shared a laugh at that. It really *did* sound a bit absurd, but also felt so right. Weird. We got quiet, lost in our own thoughts. Then, Padraig brushed the backs of his fingers against my cheek and looked me in the eyes.

"I must say I am very happy about it though. I hadn't even realized how much I had been waiting for you."

Now, *there* was a line. And then he was bending down again, and this time his kiss was more forceful, full of promise. It deepened and I found myself holding onto him, mostly to help stay standing as my knees threatened to buckle under me.

He came up for air first and gazed down at me with such a sweet smile it almost brought tears to my eyes. I don't think I realized how much I had been waiting for him, either. Fast, yes, but at a certain point I think you simply know and especially as you grow older, that point seems to come more easily. At least, I hoped it did.

Out of the corner of my eye, I saw someone walking down the road towards us and we separated, pulling out of our charged moment. We shared a glance, a bit embarrassed now by our display, and turned to see who it was. We recognized him at the same time.

"Liam!"

"Uncle Liam!"

Uncle Liam?

Padraig and I looked at each other. "You know—?" we both started to say. Liam just laughed. I suddenly remembered the odd exchange between Liam and Louise as we were leaving Riversdale House. Had he known?

He was watching my expression and seemed to read my mind. "Ah, I am sorry, lass," he began with a laugh. "I should have said something, but at first I was not sure and then it was just too much fun.

I was hoping I would see you again; see how things turned out. The way Padraig talked about you."

There it was again. He had talked about me! And apparently not wasted much time. I slid my gaze over to Padraig and found him eyeing me as well, probably to gauge my reaction and see if I was freaked out. Considering my own thoughts, and my conversations with Kathleen, I was actually a bit relieved at how he'd reacted. Maybe we really were kindred souls.

"Wait, how do you know Amelia?" Padraig's embarrassment had now turned to confusion. He looked to his uncle (I still couldn't believe it) for an answer.

"Oh, boy. I am sorry. I don't mean to be having such fun at your expense," Liam said, with a laugh. "Amelia and her friend, Kathleen, stayed at Riversdale House on the way here. They quite charmed me and the boys, but how could I be sure they were the same girls who had stayed with you?"

Charmed him and the boys? What boys, and how connected *was* this place? This was surely a bit strange, but I couldn't say I was all that bothered by it. So far I had felt a great connection with everyone I'd met. That had to be good, right?

Padraig and I responded at the same time.

"So *that's* why you mentioned stopping in Tarbert to us!"

"Is *that* why you suggested I come visit my folks?"

Liam chuckled and looked between us, obviously pleased with himself, and maybe a bit apologetic at our confusion.

"Well, anyway, you two were obviously on your way somewhere. Don't let me keep you. I was just walking into town. Might visit your folks later on today; maybe I'll see you there."

Liam continued walking down the road, turned a corner, and was gone. Okay, had that really happened? I wished I'd found my tongue faster. What if I never saw him again? Though the way things were going, I probably would.

"So, it appears you are just wiggling your way right into my life," Padraig said, and looked down at me. He raised an eyebrow in mock accusation, and then smiled as if he were quite pleased.

"Hey, I could be pretty freaked out by this too. You knew where Kathleen and I were going. You could have put people on alert." Though I was not sure why he would actually have done that.

"Well, I didn't, and I'm sure you don't really think that." It was as if he were a mind reader.

"No, I don't. I actually think it's kind of neat. A strange cosmic connection," I said, and then regretted it. No need to get too weird or push too hard and fast on this.

"I quite agree," was all he said, and he bent to kiss me again. *Sigh!*

We walked a while longer, taking in our surroundings and sharing more stories. Stories of growing up with aunts and uncles (apparently Liam was a great storyteller on Christmas Eve) and more on our siblings (his younger brother being convinced Santa Claus, the Easter Bunny, and the Tooth Fairy all knew each other; Anne and I playing jokes on people by pretending to be each other, and making him a little nervous). We even delved a bit more into college years (the awe-inspiring grounds and buildings of Trinity College and the towering trees and beautiful brick buildings of CSU Chico; Kathleen and I playing April Fool's pranks on our other roommates).

We had paused to sit on the edge of a low rock wall when we felt the first raindrop fall. Oh man, not again! Normally I loved rain, but I was starting to get nervous about making it to Doolin. Never before had weather so affected my travels.

"Well, this is just not letting up, is it?" Padraig looked down at me. "Would you like to head back into town? I was thinking of showing you my parents' house, but I'm afraid we would be soaked by the time we got there. I also don't want to make you uncomfortable by rushing anything. Meeting the parents and all that."

"Well, I *would* appreciate staying as dry as possible. Kathleen and I already got caught in the rain once this trip," I said. "Would there be another time to meet your parents?"

He gave me a wink. "Sure thing." He had just grabbed my hand to start our walk back to town when the skies opened up, accompanied by a great streak of lightning and crack of thunder. What in the world?

Padraig changed course and raced us to the cover of a grove of dense trees. All I could think was that I hoped that they, being quite tall, would act as better lightning rods than us. It was so dark I had no idea what time it actually was—we had been strolling for a while. Padraig looked down at me, probably to check my reaction to all of this, and we both broke into smiles and then laughter. He opened his arms and drew me into a great hug, both of us still laughing as we clung to each other. Anyone walking by would have thought we were nuts.

"I must say, I do love the elements," I said, as I calmed down. "Always, since I was a kid. Something about the energy of storms."

"I do too, actually," Padraig responded. "Maybe not being *out* in one," he finished, with a laugh.

"Oh, to be inside right now, by a fire with a mug of hot chocolate and slippers on."

"Oh, stop teasing," he said, and gave an involuntary shudder.

"Cold?" I asked, only teasing a bit. The temperature had dropped as well, and it had not been all that warm to begin with.

"Actually, yes," he said. "I think we should stay close together for warmth. Would not want hypothermia to set in or anything." He said this as innocently as possible, but I saw the smile trying to break through. I agreed, however, not wanting to "endanger" either of us.

We stood like that for a while, relaxed into each other and listening to the sound of the rain in the trees around us. It was still coming down pretty hard out past the protection of the trees, but we stayed relatively dry in our little spot. I became aware of the sound of his heartbeat and thought how nice this was—but so quick. I felt so close to him and wanted nothing more than to get lost in all this, but my head (with all its years of wisdom) was trying to keep *some* reality in the situation. Padraig's arms tightened a little around me, almost as if he could sense where my thoughts were going. I looked up out of curiosity.

"The rain has let up a bit, so maybe we should make a run for town now while we have the chance," Padraig said. "Getting warm sooner rather than later would be a good idea too."

I nodded in agreement but could not help feeling a little let down at having to move away from him. What a great excuse that had been! He bent and kissed the tip of my nose (reading my thoughts again?), gave me a wink, and grabbed my hand as he turned towards the road. We pretty much ran the whole way back to town, which was actually quicker than I had thought. We must have been strolling at a pretty leisurely pace on the way out.

As we came rushing up to the front door of Keldun House, two more people ran in from the opposite direction, looking decidedly wetter than us. Kathleen nearly shoved me through the door trying to get into the warmth of the lobby.

# 22

"What happened to you guys?" I asked once we were all inside. "You're soaked!"

"I know," Kathleen answered, eyeing Cian but laughing. "We took a nice scenic walk that really had no overhead coverage. It was pretty for a while ..."

"We got stuck too, but luckily there were trees to stand under," I replied. "You definitely get the first shower."

She and Cian disappeared towards the rooms rather quickly, determined to get out of their wet clothes as soon as possible. I lingered with Padraig, not wanting our time to end just yet. We decided not to sit on the chairs though, because our pants *were* a bit damp.

"Thank you for this morning," I said, suddenly feeling shy. "The breakfast wake-up, nice walk, conversation ..."

"You are quite welcome, Amelia," he replied, with a nice warmth in his voice. "I would also like to thank Mother Nature for her well-timed storm and well-placed trees." He gave me a somewhat wicked smile. I couldn't help noticing how the corners of his eyes crinkled (and becoming a bit weak in the knees). I really could be such a girl sometimes. I think I even let out a little sigh.

Mary came around the corner and saw us standing there, clothes dripping on her carpet. "Oh, you two got caught out in the storm too. I haven't seen more people running around this town. You both must be frozen. Go change before you catch your deaths, and I'll put on a pot of coffee for everyone. Cookies are already in the oven."

*Now* she was talking. We made our way to our rooms and said we would see each other in a little while. Kathleen emerged, saying she needed coffee ASAP and the place was all mine. A nice warm shower sounded so good, and then some alone time to call Anne.

I turned my face up and enjoyed the warmth of the water as it streamed down my body. I was totally relaxed, as in my bones were like jelly, but could not help feeling excited as well by the events of the morning. Being so close to Padraig and the kiss. I felt the big cheesy grin on my face, but did not care. Besides, no one could see me.

Deciding to not get too lost in thought, lest I drain the building of warm water, I focused on lathering my hair, sudsing up and rinsing off. I stepped out of the shower with regret. I really could have stayed in there much longer—and that was generally where I did my best thinking. Why, I did not know.

I dressed quickly in warm (but cute) clothes and sat on my bed to call Anne. I grabbed my cell phone off the night stand, punched in her number, and waited. She answered on the second ring.

"*Where* have you been? Where are you guys?"

Oops. Guess I had waited too long. "Sorry, Anne. I meant to call sooner. We're still here, and there's a pretty good storm going on right now so I'm assuming we won't be going anywhere today."

"Oh, no." Anne was upset, but she seemed fairly calm considering. "James and the boys are golfing at La Hinch for his bachelor party right now. I hope it doesn't move north and cut their day short, though I'm sure they would stay out in any case."

"Or spend the extra time in the clubhouse with Irish coffees," I said with a laugh.

"Yeah, that would be a good move too," she agreed.

"Oh, Anne—I'm so sorry about all this. We'll get there in time to help with the plans and give you a proper bachelorette party. As Kathleen pointed out, you'll need time to recover."

She laughed and expressed her agreement, then started chattering on about the different wedding details that were coming together. She had found a wonderful lady to help her with fresh flowers—delivering and setting up for the day of. I listened intently and got wrapped up in her enthusiasm, but then I had to share my news before I burst with it.

"So—some things have been happening to make our delay more enjoyable," I began.

"*What?* What is it?" She knew right away from my tone that it was something big.

"Well, Kathleen may be staying here, and I've met someone."

There was only silence from the other end of the phone. I had laid it all out at once for dramatic effect. My sister and I loved shocking each other, since it was such a rare feat. The whole twin connect and all that.

"I'm sorry. It sounded like you just said that Kathleen was staying here and that you had met someone."

"I'm not kidding," I rushed on. "Oh, I've wanted to talk to you so bad. This has been insane but so exciting!" I let out a little squeal.

"What! Tell me, tell me!"

"Ohhh ... Okay, so his name is Padraig. He's the hotel manager at Baggot Court and I met him on our first day here. I don't know—we just clicked. At least for me. I've just been so taken with this guy, Anne! We kept running into each other, and Kathleen and I hung out with him and his friends one night. He's just so easy to talk to, and I really like being with him. He kissed me too, and it was just amazing. I haven't felt this way for so long, and it's really, really nice." I finally paused to take a deep breath.

"So ... My gawd! ... You sound so happy and lit up. I love that! Knowing you, you've already thought of this and worried about it, but what happens in a few days? When you leave and he stays, I'm assuming."

"I know, I know—and yes—you know me. I *have* thought of that, and we both decided to just enjoy this and see where it goes. Very unlike me, I know, but I just want to get wrapped up in it, Anne. Is that so wrong?" I paused. "Could I get my heart broken? Yes. But I think I'm ready to stop thinking and analyzing so much."

"First of all, *no* it's not wrong. Who says there's a certain right way to meet and connect with people? You've been cautious since your last relationship; you've analyzed yourself; time to move on. Second, I'm proud of you for opening up to the risk. I think we need to be out of our comfort zone every now and again. And you never know."

"Yeah, that's what Kathleen keeps saying."

"Well, she is a very smart girl. I *knew* I liked her." We both giggled at that. "And you mentioned something about Kathleen too? What the heck? You guys have been busy!"

"*Dude* you will not believe this. Remember that cute musician she ran into, literally, at Thing Mote a couple years ago?"

"Uh-huh—that fiddle player—and they danced all night and she regretted not seeing him again or trying to find him before she left?"

"That's the one! Well, his name is Cian. He's a singer too now, and we ran into him in a little pub in Graiguenamanagh; and she now wants to stay in Ireland to be his band's manager and partner in life."

"*What!*"

"Okay, not so much that last part, but they are pretty inseparable, and I would not be surprised if it went that way. Something has definitely rekindled, and she is quite smitten."

"Well, well. Jeez, you guys know how to have a proper holiday! I miss all the good stuff." I could almost see her pout on the other end of the phone. "So, will I get to meet these gentlemen? Are they coming to the wedding?"

"Oh, that's the best part. Cian's band is playing at your wedding!" She burst out laughing on her end of the line. "How did that happen, by the way? You'll need to tell me later—so random! But I hadn't thought of inviting Padraig. Do you think that would be a good idea? Do you mind?"

"Are you kidding? The first guy who turns my sister's head in I don't know how long? Uh, yes. I need to meet him."

"Well, alrighty then. I guess I'd better go ask him."

We talked for a bit longer, mostly her gushing about different wedding details and how well things were coming along. I promised to get there as soon as I could (hopefully by the next day), and then she shooed me off the phone to get back to Padraig. What a nice change, I couldn't help thinking. All three of us with men to entertain—and be entertained by.

# 23

The first thing I saw in the dining room was actually a person—Padraig—looking so crazy cute I couldn't stand it. His hair was still a little damp from his shower, and it curled a bit more than usual around his temples and neck. He also had on a cozy-looking dark brown fisherman sweater that matched his hair color and looked extremely huggable. The second thing I saw was a steaming mug of coffee at an empty chair next to him, presumably waiting for me. So thoughtful.

When he looked up and saw me, his face broke into a smile, and he stood up to pull my chair out (again!). He also placed a soft kiss on the side of my temple, and I felt my insides flutter. Oh my, I could *really* get used to this. The only problem with enjoying this and seeing where it went, was that I *knew* where I wanted it to go. Tricky.

"For you," he said, gesturing to the coffee.

"Thank you, this is so nice," I said, as I wrapped my hands around the mug to warm them. Good, then it was not for Gwynn. I couldn't help the glance I had thrown around the room when I came in and saw the mug sitting there. "So, question."

Padraig looked at me quizzically as he took a long swallow of coffee. "Please," was all he said, but did he look a little nervous?

"I just got off the phone with my sister, and she would like you to be my guest at the wedding. What do you say? Are you free?" Okay, now I was getting a bit nervous. Was this pushing it? What if it was too fast and he said no?

"That sounds great," he said, instantly putting my fears to rest. "I'd really like to meet this sister I keep hearing so much about. I took some days off from Baggot Court to be here anyway, so I'm all yours."

He seemed genuinely pleased that I had asked, and I could not help smiling back at him as he spoke. Was this guy for real, and had he really been sent just for me? I couldn't have dreamed up someone better, and I really did not want to think about having to give him up in just a few days. Enough with the thinking, I chastised myself. Sheesh!

"Padraig!"

I knew that voice. Oh, crap. I looked up and saw Gwynn. I had spoken too soon. (Well, thought.) Here she was, after all. She saw me then, and I swear I saw her face fall. But she refocused on Padraig and was all sunshine and smiles again. What a strange reality to be faced with, and so quickly. I had just met this guy and was still trying to come to terms with my sudden feelings, and I was already being thrown into the good old-fashioned jealousy scenario.

"Gwynn. Wow, twice in one day," Padraig said, as she approached. "What's the occasion? Doesn't your own hotel need you?"

I sensed a little tension in his voice. Maybe even a little irritation? Oh good, so all these interruptions were maybe not so welcome after all. Her face did drop a bit at his words. She knew him well enough that she would probably be able to read that better than I. She tried to recover quickly, though, and sat with us at our table (again).

"Oh, you." Now she was trying to be coy. "My hotel is a well-oiled machine, and I often take breaks during the day to drop in on Mom. Have a bit of a chat, see if she needs any help with anything." She finally slid her glance over and acknowledged me. "Hello again, Amelia. Sorry, I did not mean to be rude. Did you both enjoy your walk? I assume you got caught out in the rain with the rest of the town."

"Yes, we sure did," I said, tossing in a laugh. "It was great, though. Padraig showed me some beautiful countryside, and we had a good amount of time before the rain really started in on us."

"Oh, and get this," Padraig jumped in. "We ran into my Uncle Liam, and Amelia knows him. Old codger had way too much fun with us. She and her friend stayed at his place in Glendalough for a couple nights on the way here. Funny, huh."

She did seem interested by this and laughed with us. Such a trip, this girl was. When she pulled the claws in, she seemed lovely.

"He was quite taken with her," Padraig continued. He looked at me with a bit of affection, almost as if he were proud. I felt a nice glow under the attention, but it proved too much for Gwynn.

"Well, I should go find Mom before I have to head back," she said, and stood up. "How long are you staying here?" This was directed at Padraig.

"I'm actually cutting it a bit short, as I have just been invited to join Amelia at her sister's wedding," he said, and placed his arm across the back of my chair. "We'll head across on the ferry as soon as we can—hopefully tomorrow."

"Ah," was her only response, and a darkness seemed to come over her face. "Well, you better say goodbye before you go. I never see you now that you're in Dublin." Gwynn said this as almost an accusation, and I felt like I was intruding on something private.

"Sure," was his easy response. Either he'd missed her tone or was ignoring it.

She turned then and left the room, which was decidedly chillier than when I first entered. Next to me, Padraig seemed thoughtful. It was probably none of my business, but I could not stay quiet.

"She seems to miss you," I observed. He looked at me for a moment, maybe trying to decide how much to say, and slowly nodded.

"We were very close growing up, and in a small town that really means something," he finally said. "I was more her older brother—looked out for her and all that."

"Well, you must have done a very good job."

"Ah, well, we all have to grow up eventually. Not everyone is meant to stay in a small town forever." He gave me a little smile to lighten the mood, then went back to his coffee.

"So." I tried to think of something to switch tracks. "With my last-minute invitation, do you have anything to wear to the wedding? It's totally fine whatever you have; you could even wear what you have on now."

"Well, this is your lucky day. Or mine, actually. You just happened to ask me in the town where my parents live, and my only suit just happens to be at their house. So, a quick visit there before we leave, and I'm all set."

I gave him a genuine smile at that. This was going to be so much fun! We talked more about the wedding as we continued to warm up.

"So, you get to meet my parents as well." I finally threw it out there. "How do you feel about that? Too soon?"

He gave me a reassuring smile. "I think I can handle it and would be honored to meet them. You already know my uncle. I have some catching up to do." He winked.

We heard a ruckus at the door and looked up to see Kathleen and Cian come piling into the room. I realized the rest of the band had been in there with us all along, also enjoying the treats Mary had set out. So, where had those two been?

"Well, what is this?" Padraig asked with mock sternness, like a big brother checking up on Kathleen. "Where have you two been, and why are you all wet again after having come in to dry off ..." He trailed off and raised an eyebrow, making all of us break into laughter.

Kathleen collapsed into the chair next to me and tried to catch her breath. Cian stayed where he was, leaning against the doorframe.

"I swear ..." Kathleen struggled to reply, "we thought we could make it. There was a dry spot in the weather ..."

Was she *trying* to make sense? We all continued watching her, waiting to hear the story.

"Started raining again ..." she panted. "*Lightning*!"

Cian just stood there, looking quite pale, actually. Then they both started to laugh—somewhat hysterically—I suppose at whatever had just happened to them. The rest of us gave up and went back to our own conversations, letting them keep their strange moment to themselves.

"So," I said to Kathleen as she continued to collect herself and seemed to be calming down. "I've asked Padraig to come to the wedding, and he's accepted. Now we both have dates," I finished happily, then glanced a bit shyly at Padraig.

"Oh, that's great!" Kathleen looked happily at both of us in turn. "We can all caravan together. Cian and the guys are wanting to be there as soon as possible to work on logistics, and they'll be with us on the first ferry across."

"Speaking of—" Padraig broke into the conversation. "I should be getting that suit we were talking about sooner rather than later. It could take a bit of time, and we want to be ready to jump at a moment's notice to get you to your sister." He gave me a nudge, and stood up to leave the table.

"Are you sure? I could go with you. Help somehow—"

"Oh, no, that's fine. You stay here and relax, warm and dry. I'll be back as soon as I can." With that, he was gone.

I tried to keep thoughts of Gwynn out of my mind, but it was hard. And not meeting his parents, though he *had* mentioned it before we were caught in the rain. Just my mind running away. *Stop it!*

I turned back to Kathleen who regarded me curiously. I really didn't want to go into it right then, so I started telling her about my conversation with Anne. She seemed happy that I'd connected with my sister and let her know where we were. By this time Cian and the guys had retreated to their room, so I had her full attention. Just me and my best friend, cozy and snug in a wonderful little bed and breakfast, and exactly as I had imagined when we started this trip. In that moment I felt very lucky—as if I were exactly where I was meant to be.

Kathleen realized she hadn't spoken to Anne at all since being in Ireland and insisted I call her back. I happened to have my phone in my pocket, so we called her from our table in the dining room. She answered quickly, and I told her she was on speakerphone.

"Is Kathleen there too, then?"

"Yes! Hi, Anne. It's good to hear your voice!"

There was a squeal from the other end of the phone, and Kathleen and I joined in.

"*Kathleen,* I finally get to talk to you! How *are* you? After all I've been hearing ... Oh, you guys feel so close now. I get to see you soon, right?"

"That is the plan," I said. "Quite a few folks are getting antsy here, so hopefully the ferries can find a way to open tomorrow."

"And you both have dates. My gawd. How did this happen so fast? And how did I miss it?"

Kathleen laughed at my sister's tone. "Believe me, we certainly did not see any of this coming. I still can't quite believe it, to tell you the truth. My head is spinning. So how *did* you manage to book Cian and the guys? And how did you not recognize him and tell me?"

"To be honest, I had nothing to do with it. The band was recommended to James by a friend, and he wanted to do his part with the planning, so he did it all himself. That's *hilarious,* though. I can't wait to tell him."

"Where is James?" I jumped in. "Has he made it back from La Hinch yet?"

"No, and it's pouring rain here too. Last I talked to him, he and the boys were at the clubhouse like you said." She laughed. "That was about an hour ago, so we'll see when I see him. They got all the holes in though, so he was happy. Time to relax anyway."

"Oh, that's good. So what have you been doing all this time? I'm assuming the others are there by now?"

"Yeah, Michelle and Marie got here yesterday and Mom and Dad are here now. Everyone is so excited and can't wait for you two to get here. We just can't start properly celebrating without you."

"I know, I know. We're trying. *Oh*, and can you share with us yet which bridesmaid dress you chose? We're dying to know what we get to be excited about wearing!"

"Oh, right." She sounded excited, so I figured we'd be happy. "I still want those to be a surprise for you all, but I *can* tell you they're a treat from me and James. A bit of a thank you, especially with everyone having to buy plane tickets."

"*Omigosh!*" Kathleen and I squealed again.

"That's so nice, sister," I continued. "You *did* stick with the color that compliments my complexion though, right?" I couldn't help teasing.

"I actually found the one that looked the ugliest on me, and that was the one I chose," she teased back. "It *is* my day, after all."

"Yeah, yeah."

"Okay, sis. I better get going. Mom is waiting to show me something. Call when you guys are leaving or in the morning, whichever comes first?"

I promised I would, and we hung up. I turned to Kathleen. "So she's sticking to her surprise."

"And treating us!" Kathleen added. "How nice for my bank account."

I nodded.

"She probably picked orange just to screw with me. Anything goes with brown hair, so you have nothing to worry about."

I pictured orange with Kathleen's reddish hair and laughed. "She wouldn't do that," I assured my friend as we stood and walked toward the hall. Somehow, we'd silently agreed to head back to our room. I loved our brains.

We flopped down on our beds, and I thought again how nice it was to be with my friend for a while.

"Hey, did you see that girl in the dining room this morning?"

"The blonde sitting with Padraig?" Kathleen replied. "Who didn't?"

I sat straight up on my bed, instantly alert. "She was beautiful, right? It wasn't just me being paranoid and insecure? Do you think Padraig thinks so?"

"I wouldn't say that." She reluctantly pulled herself up to a sitting position. "I know where your head is going, and don't go there. I saw nothing untoward, at least not on his end. Besides, it's far too early for head-trips and whack-outs."

"But there was something on her end; am I right?" I pressed.

"Yes, I suppose there was. She seemed—attentive—but who knows. He said they were old friends, right? So there will be a closeness, but he didn't look at her like he looked at you. Besides, you don't want to seem all possessive and jealous right off the bat. Talk about scaring him away before you even have a chance to figure out where the relationship will go next."

Of course Kathleen was right, and I loved that she knew me so well and gave it to me straight. I laid back down with a sigh. "I know. Of course, you're right. He *did* give me a kiss right in front of her," I said, with a wicked grin.

"I noticed that," Kathleen replied, and gave a small chuckle.

"So, what happened to you and Cian this afternoon?" I was still curious.

"Oh." She laughed, but flushed and seemed a bit embarrassed. "The guys were in the room, and we wanted to be alone so we went outside for a bit ..." She trailed off, and I could only imagine what they'd been doing. "Anyway," she continued, "it had been clearing, but then it started pouring again and lightning struck a tree near us and broke a branch off. Gawd, it was so loud and scared the pants off us. We ran back as fast as we could in case another strike came, and well, that's when you saw us. I guess we panicked and went straight for the dining room, not thinking everyone would be there." She shook her head and laughed again, and I joined in.

"Your faces were priceless. I wonder if Cian has any color back in his yet." I laughed again, and now I was on a roll. Soon we were both doubled over, gasping for air. I wiped tears away and tried to calm down, sitting up straighter in bed. Kathleen came over and sat on my bed, putting her arm across my shoulders.

"I'm so glad we did this. I'm so glad to be here with you. Thank you for the idea to rent a car and travel around."

"I agree, my friend, and you're quite welcome." I hugged her back. "It worked out well for us, didn't it?"

"I would say so," she answered with a solemn nod.

"Well then. What shall we do now?" I posed the question to the room at large. Rain beat against our window, making us cozy inside, but also making me wonder about ferry conditions for the next day. Kathleen managed to read my mind.

"Good news is, Cian and I overheard some fishermen talking by the docks and they said this storm is supposed to blow out by tonight. Clear skies tomorrow, and the ferries should start back up."

"You don't say! Well, that is good news."

"So, what was with Padraig? Something about getting a suit?"

"Oh, yeah. He wants to look nice for the wedding, and he keeps one at his parents' house. So, he went to get it."

"You guys had your own fun today. What did you do, anyway?"

"Well ... he took me on a walk towards the outskirts of town and actually was taking me to see his parents' house when the rain started.

We didn't get very far, but he asked if I wanted to meet them. He wanted me to meet them!"

"And he'll meet yours in just a couple days. Oh my, this *is* getting serious." She gave me a look.

"Shut up! Don't you dare give me a complex now. This was your idea!"

"I know," she said simply. "It was just too good to pass up."

"*Oh,* and get this. We ran into Liam! You know, from Riversdale House? He's Padraig's uncle! I mean, can this get any freakier? And apparently Liam knew who we were, or at least suspected, from whatever Padraig had been saying to him. Kind of cute, right? Please tell me that's cute and not just plain weird."

"No, no. Definitely cute." She laughed and shook her head. "You're kidding me though! That's great. I wonder when I'll meet random Cian people."

"Hey, I think Cian is quite enough. I mean—a chance encounter, then a few years later—reunited? That just doesn't happen."

"I know. And it happened to me!" She hugged herself and swayed back and forth.

A knock at the door caused Kathleen to pause mid-sway. She actually froze, as if someone could see her and this would make her invisible. I gave her a look and went to open the door. It was Mary.

"Hello, dear. I am sorry to bother you. Oh, hello, Kathleen!" Our host peeked in and waved at Kathleen, then continued directing the conversation towards me. "You have a phone call—Padraig is on the phone for you."

*A phone call? For me? Here? How weird was this.*

"Come, you can take it at the desk."

I followed Mary into the hallway, glancing back at Kathleen and meeting her questioning gaze. Well, this was certainly a new travel experience.

When I got to the desk, Mary went around to the other side, took the phone off the cradle, and handed it to me.

"Hello? Padraig?" Oh this was so weird—but kind of familiar too.

"Amelia? I hope I'm not alarming you with my call."

*Yes, you are actually. There is a storm that you went out in, and should be back by now, and you're calling me instead.* "No, not at all. Everything all right? Did you get your suit?"

"Yes, I have it right here and I'm still at my folks' house. I was about to leave when Gwynn stopped by ..."

Alarm bells went off in my head. *Gwynn?* Again? What in the— Padraig was still talking, so I tried to tune back in.

"Anyway, it looks like I'll be here a little while longer, so I didn't want you to worry. And please, go ahead and eat with Kathleen and everyone else. Dinner should be coming soon, and I am sure you'll be hungry."

I was pretty sure I wouldn't be.

"I'll find you when I get back. Hopefully I won't be here too long. I wish I were there with you."

I'm not sure exactly what my response was but we got off the phone amicably, and I hung up in a bit of a daze. This was getting— problematic. Mary was watching me and looked concerned, so I gave her a small smile and turned away from the desk. I made my way back to our room, where I relayed the conversation to Kathleen.

"Well, at least he called you to explain. That was very considerate. And he wishes he was here, right? But I agree. That Gwynn is getting downright annoying."

I was happy to have my friend on my side and told her so. This was really starting to get to me. I mean, relationships were hard enough— especially when they were starting out and trying to gain footing. To attempt it from two different continents—when the foot-gaining had to happen in just a week's time—well, that was starting to seem crazy to me.

"Oh, no. You're thinking, aren't you?" My friend knew me too well. Of course, it might have been a give-away that I was pacing and giving myself a headache from scowling so hard.

"How can I help it? I'm already encountering crazy bitch drama that you only really see in the movies, and it's just a few days in. And I am *not* looking forward to having to have the what-happens-when-I-leave-for-home conversation."

"I know, I know." She sat down on her bed, seeming at a loss for words and ideas to help. "Let's just go have some dinner with the guys and see what happens when Padraig gets back."

I agreed, because I had no energy to argue or think of anything else. We walked back down the hallway towards the dining room (something *did* smell really good) and found some smiling familiar faces already waiting for us. Kathleen was decidedly happier than I was; but hey, it was her due too.

The table was full of conversation and laughter (and maybe even a little flirting from Gerry the drummer), and normally I would have been pulled right in. Not tonight. The food was wonderful (meatloaf and vegetables), and I actually felt a stab of guilt that I hadn't helped Mary as I had the night before. But that was a special circumstance, I told myself. Mary normally did this herself.

We moved through dinner, and then dessert and coffee. Still no Padraig. Now I was getting a little worried, though did I really have a right to be? Conversations died, and people started excusing themselves from the table. The dining room as a whole had begun to clear out. I sat as long as I could, Kathleen casting worried glances in my direction, but finally I had to give in to tiredness and got ready to follow Kathleen back to the room.

I was just leaving when Mary popped her head out of the kitchen and called me over. Well, this was curious. I stopped in front of her with a "Hi, Mary" that I hoped didn't sound as cautious as I felt. I tried for a convincing smile.

"Look, there is something I want to share with you." She started right in. "My daughter ..." Gwynn! Oh, here it came. "She can be a bit—single-minded. Ever since she was a little girl, she's had a thing for Padraig. Always the handsomest boy in town, looked after her, kept bullies away from her. He never returned it, mind you. Always saw her as a younger sibling, a nuisance even." Mary smiled at some memory. "I only tell you this because I see she's been visiting here lately and paying a good amount of attention to Padraig since he's been back in town.

"I love my daughter, but she does not always have the right of it and I want Padraig to be happy. You make him happy." She patted my shoulder. "Besides, I like you too. You're a good sort. I know you're only visiting, but you seem quite natural here. You never quite know what could happen." She smiled at me then. "Now, go on, off to bed, and don't give it another thought. I'll have a chat with Padraig when he gets in, and I know he will. I'll make sure of that." She gave me a wink, and then shooed me down the hallway and off to bed.

I couldn't help noticing the hint of worry that stayed in her eyes as she smiled. I did feel better, though, and gave her a shy smile in return. Sometimes people came into your life for a reason—they really did. I turned and headed back to the room, my mind swirling with all sorts of thoughts.

It was only around eight o'clock, but it was so dark and quiet outside that it felt nice being inside and tucked in for the night. I didn't even hear much noise from the rain, so maybe Kathleen and the fishermen were right.

I walked into the room and just stared at Kathleen. She stared right back with a *So? Tell me!* expression. I sat on the end of my bed and smiled.

"That was so strange—and great."

I relayed my conversation with Mary, deciding to keep my unease to myself. My friend listened with great interest and shook her head or nodded at the appropriate times. When I finished, she sat back and shook her head.

"Well, you've made some very good friends, missy. She really sided against her own daughter for you."

"I know. I was pretty floored too. And flattered. And telling me I should stay, like some mystic who can read my thoughts? *But*—I was right. Was I not?"

"Yes, you were right. Woman's intuition wins again." She laughed lightly and shook her head. "Crazy. Well, I hope you feel better. And I think we should get some sleep. Nothing wrong with being up and ready and packed when those ferries open tomorrow."

"I agree. Absolutely."

I really did too. I could not help feeling just a little anxious still, but Mary had really calmed me down. Amazing—the help you could get when and from where you least expected it.

We slowly got ready for bed, Kathleen playing music on her phone to make it all the more fun. I found myself dancing around the room and actually enjoying it, letting loose as I played a monster riff on her hairbrush or sang a particularly impassioned line into my toothbrush. We settled after a few minutes and tucked ourselves into bed, putting our heads to our pillows, ready to get fully relaxed. I drifted off to sleep, realizing that I was listening for the sound of Padraig entering the building. It did not come.

# 24

I woke up the next morning to the sound of Kathleen's voice. "Am, you have to see this."

She was standing by the door, staring down at a little piece of white paper on the floor. "I think it's for you."

I picked the paper up and unfolded it with Kathleen hovering over my shoulder.

Amelia~

I'm so sorry I did not come back last night as I said I would. The situation was a little more complicated and needed more attention than I had originally thought. I will explain more in the morning if you would like to hear it. I hope you had a good evening and a sweet sleep. I'll be in the dining room waiting when you wake.

XOXO
Padraig

XOXO! Well, that was certainly a nice way to wake up. Kathleen was still behind me, grinning from ear to ear.

"Not too bad. Not too bad at all. Mary must have really given him an earful."

I nodded and laughed. "I do hope he's okay."

She gave me a look and walked into the bathroom. "I'll be quick. I'm sure you'll want to move through here as fast as possible."

I gave her a grateful smile and she gave me a knowing one back. She even gave me a good smack on the rear and then disappeared into the bathroom.

I couldn't keep the smile off my face as I sank onto my bed and reread the note. Very thoughtful indeed. I could see him writing this without any help from Mary, and that was the best part. I had to stop myself from running down the hall, throwing myself at him, and giving him a big hug. But, no—I wanted to look my best. And maybe letting him sweat a little didn't hurt either.

Kathleen had told the truth. She was in and out before I could even pick out clothes to wear. I rushed into the bathroom, eager to get the day started. (This could be the day we made it across and joined the wedding, finally!) But I did decide to take a quick shower to be ready for whatever it might hold.

I put the finishing touches on my makeup, grabbed a sweater, and headed out the door. Kathleen had decided to stay in the room to give Padraig and me as much privacy as possible. It was seven (I wondered if this early wake-up call would stay, back in San Francisco), so that might not have been too hard.

I walked down the now very familiar hallway and stood inside the dining room door. I saw Padraig before he saw me. It looked like he had not slept much at all. He looked sleepy and rumpled, though in different clothes than the day before, and I immediately *did* want to hug him. My heart went out to him, and any anxious thoughts I'd had were instantly gone. In that moment, I realized I was really starting to fall for this guy—which was a little scary—but exciting too.

He looked up and saw me, and his face transformed. Where there had been a somewhat defeated look spread one of joy and warmth. It almost seemed as if a light had been turned on inside him.

He stood up as though he was going to walk towards me, but I rushed up and threw my arms around him (just like I'd said I would).

He closed me in a tight hug, and I breathed a little sigh of relief. I suppose I *had* still been a bit worried about him.

"Look, Amelia, I am so sorry—"

"Padraig, I was so worried—"

"You first," Padraig said.

"Oh, I was just a little worried, that's all. Probably an overreaction, but with the storm and all. I was so happy to receive your note. Thank you. That was very thoughtful."

"Yes, well ... Oh, here. Sit, sit." He motioned to a chair close to us as if he had just remembered we were still standing. We sat down, and he continued. "I understand you spoke with Mary last night. She pounced on me when I came in—well, after calling the house to see when I would be back. Said something about locking up and not wanting to lock me out." He paused as if trying to figure something out, then shook his head and went on.

"Anyway, she was right. Her daughter—you remember Gwynn?—well, she showed up at my parent's house quite upset; something about a boy she had dated and it spun into all sorts of places. Not sure why she wouldn't come here to see Mary. Anyway, she had the entire house a bit frazzled. My mother especially. Gwynn always did know how to get worked up about things. Something Mary knows all too well, and I believe actually called her to talk her into coming here. Suddenly, Gwynn up and left, saying she had somewhere else to be and was feeling much better. I grabbed my suit and came straight back. She wasn't here when I returned though, thank goodness.

"Anyway, that's what kept me. I would have much rather been here, relaxing and eating dinner with you all. You especially," he concluded, looking deep into my eyes.

Oh, how did he do that? Some nice words and an endearing smile and I was putty in his hands. Well, thank you, Mary. It sounded like she really had put in some help, and on behalf of a relative stranger no less.

It also made me start to wonder about Gwynn. Such a beauty and seemingly confident, but emotionally unstable? Interesting.

"Well, I'm certainly happy to see you." I smiled and patted his knee. "And, yes, I suppose I did have some worry on my face that Mary saw. She is a wonderful lady, I must say. Knows how to say just the right things." I would not reveal the entirety of our talk (like perhaps my real worry about Padraig and Gwynn—jealousy bordering on distrust?), and my abbreviated synopsis was certainly the truth. "You seem to have had a special world growing up here, from what I have seen so far. The area, the people ... I've enjoyed seeing a bit of where you came from."

"And I hope to see a bit of where *you* came from."

*Well!*

"You already have. Meeting Kathleen, I mean. And soon you'll meet Anne, another huge part. Then, my folks ... But, yes." I gave him a small smile. "Perhaps a little closer to home would be nice." Were we really talking about this? I think a giggle almost bubbled up out of me, that maybe would have bordered on hysterical. Him coming to San Francisco? Hmm ...

Voices started floating down the hallway—a good time to break the intensity that had built between us. Padraig leaned away from me, though it seemed reluctant. I offered to get us some of the now infamous (in my eyes, anyway) oatmeal and was at the serving table when Kathleen arrived. Her eyes zeroed in on me right away, and she made a beeline. I tried to appear casual in case Padraig noticed us, acting as if I had not spent half the evening complaining to her.

She stood next to me, pouring herself a mug of coffee and gathering her own bowl of oatmeal. To her credit, she was doing a good job at nonchalance. I also noticed that Cian was not with her.

"So?"

"So ..." I matched her lowered voice. "Mary came through. Things are fine. Great even." I couldn't help the smile that then broke across my face. Kathleen eyed me, but didn't comment.

"Well, good. I'm glad. For *his* sake."

Uh-oh. I knew I'd created some drama in bringing up my thoughts on Gwynn and my reaction to her, and I didn't want my hasty overreactions to affect my hopefully budding relationship.

We joined Padraig at the table. She was staying close to me, I realized, and I had to say I appreciated it. It was nice having her near as I navigated this new—whatever it was. Padraig didn't seem to mind, either, wishing her a good morning and making small talk. I was sure he knew how much we'd talked. I mean, what close girlfriends didn't? Any savvy gentleman would be aware of that.

Out of the corner of my eye, I noticed Cian enter the room and go over to his band's table. Then, he approached us with a smile on his face.

"Good news, everyone. The ferries are under preparations to open. Nothing official yet, but I was just at the dock talking to some workers. They said maybe another hour or so."

"Great! Yeah!" Kathleen grinned to the table at large. "No offense, Padraig, you have a lovely town here, but I am *so* ready to move on with this trip. We have some wedding celebrations to partake in."

"Hey, no offense taken. I am rather excited myself."

We dug into our breakfast with renewed gusto and were soon back in our rooms, getting ready for our departure. Kathleen and I spent the next hour packing up our belongings and predicting the shape Anne would be in when we got there. Kathleen thought she would be fairly relaxed, with preparations behind her and knowing things were moving forward with us finally there. But I knew my sister would still be a little tense. What had built up over the past few days would not have gone away quite that quickly. Some drinks at whatever pubs we found for her bachelorette night would help, though—we agreed on that.

# 25

We stood outside of Keldun House, saying goodbye to Mary, our hostess and newfound friend, and promising to visit again soon. With hugs all around, we hopped into our respective cars, ready to drive over to the ferries and hopefully be among the first to cross. Gwynn was nowhere to be seen, which was just fine by me, though at one point I thought a curtain moved slightly where no guest would be. I was still wary of her, as if we hadn't experienced the last of her antics, but was trying to push back those thoughts.

Instead, I was thinking what a good thing it was that Kathleen and I had upgraded to a larger rental car—giving us room for another passenger—much to my delight. Padraig offered to drive, since he knew these roads so well, which was a nice added benefit. Kathleen was enjoying the backseat, taking in all the scenery and probably trying to catch glimpses of Cian in the car behind us. I rode shotgun. This *really* gave me a chance to enjoy the scenery. I had an especially nice view of Padraig's strong hand and wrist as he gripped the gear stick. Man—what was it with me and his hands?

We found a line of cars waiting to board the ferry. There were quite a few people, so it looked like I'd been right. This town was going to clear out in just a little while. As we waited, Kathleen tried to think up some road trip games and Padraig played with the radio to give us some tunes. He discovered our CD in the slot and, when he pushed play, "I Wanna Be Bad" came on. How was it always that song? Padraig cast a sideways look at me. He didn't say anything, but a smile played on his lips.

Kathleen chose that time to pipe in from the backseat. "Amelia made this as our driving CD. Isn't that great?"

"Terrific," he said, eyeing me again.

"Oh, come on. It's not all girly music. There's some good stuff on there."

"Thank you, Kathleen," I said. "I did try my very hardest, and originally I thought *only girls* would be listening to it."

"All right. All right." Padraig laughed. "Fair enough."

No more was said about the CD, and I even caught Padraig moving his head to the next couple of songs. Before long we were on our way, following the car in front of us onto the ferry. No matter how many of these I had been on, it still felt a little thrilling to be able to just drive onto a boat.

We sat in companionable silence for a bit, and then started talking about the wedding and what it might entail. Kathleen and I had fun telling Padraig who all would be in attendance and various inside stories. Before we knew it, we were across the river. Hallelujah. I had been starting to think this day would never come. I pulled out my cell phone to call Anne and tell her that we were officially across. I think the entire vehicle heard her enthusiastic response.

I was still grinning at her outburst when I hung up the phone. I stole a sideways glance and noticed Padraig looking at me. I'm sure I turned bright red at the embarrassment of getting caught, but he seemed to think nothing of it and turned back to look out the windshield.

We let the music play and occasionally someone would sing along with a song. Padraig was especially excited when U2 came on. I think it gave him a new respect for my CD. He also had good control of the driving, and it was nice not to be constantly glued to a map to avoid getting lost. We made small talk here and there, even sharing initial ideas on how to surprise Anne with her bachelorette party (she was so observant and liked being in control), and just generally had a pleasant drive to the next stage of the adventure.

# 26

We pulled into Doolin from a side road—and there was Anne. I couldn't believe it. What timing! She looked to be coming out of a store. I could tell Padraig had spotted her too, because, well. She looked like me.

I rolled down my window and shouted her name. Her head whipped up and she instantly zeroed in on us. Luckily she was only carrying a small bag, because she sprinted for the car. Literally sprinted. She came to a stop directly in front of the hood (thankfully no one was coming up behind us) and shrieked something unintelligible, but sounded something like *"Omigawd, you're heeeerrre!"* I thought I saw her eyes sweep briefly across Padraig before she was around to my side of the car and hugging me through the window. Behind me, Kathleen was bouncing in her seat and screaming too. I could only imagine what Padraig must be thinking.

"Take a left onto the road," she directed. "We're all staying at Cullinan's. There are parking spaces," she added. "We can get you guys settled and then come back out and play!"

Padraig did as instructed while I sat in the passenger seat grinning from ear to ear. It was so good to be here and finally back with my sister. The day was clear and beautiful, and I found myself wondering if James was back at La Hinch giving it another try.

We found the hotel in no time, and Anne was there (had she run?) and ready with hugs and help with bags. She greeted Padraig rather solemnly, and I tried to shoot warnings into the back of her head to be nice. He handled it well, though, and played along, and soon they were fast friends. He even asked if he could chaperone her bachelorette party if it happened.

*Shoot!* I had almost forgotten. But with the wedding in two days, we could still give her a proper evening tonight and have tomorrow to recover. Perfect. I'd have to talk with Michelle and Marie, the two bridesmaids who were already in town.

Anne helped us check in and unpack, then we went back out to explore town. She showed us her favorite stores and restaurants and we ended up at O'Connor's pub, where we met up with the rest of the group, including James and the boys, who were there after all. The excitement was palpable. After hugs all around, Anne and I excused ourselves to get a round of drinks at the bar and some much-needed sister time—her squeals over Padraig, my gushes on how radiant she looked.

Kathleen came over to join the reunion and help carry drinks back. I took one for Padraig and sat next to him at the large table, a bit beside myself that he was really here with me and that all that had gone on had really gone on. Every so often we shared a private look, and it was nice to see he was truly enjoying himself. He had no trouble jumping into conversation and hit it off quite well with James and his friends.

When I excused myself to the bathroom, I made meaningful eye contact with Michelle, Marie, and Kathleen. We hatched a plan to "kidnap" Anne that evening (as in blindfolded from her room) and come for a nice pub crawl as her proper end to single life. On our way back to the table, we tried not to look too suspicious, though I saw Anne eyeing us all in turn. I just smiled back innocently and asked where Mom and Dad were. That did it.

Her face fell—as if she had forgotten something. "Oh, they were going to look for something for me! I wonder if they found it ..." She pulled out her cell phone and dialed a number, at the same time excusing herself from the table. Padraig saw all this and seemed more than a little impressed by my deception. I must say, I was a little impressed myself.

Padraig slipped his hand over mine, and I swore I saw Michelle's and Marie's eyes widen. I wondered how much Anne had said to them. Michelle had been Anne's best friend since elementary school and Marie was a good friend from teaching, so I could see her telling them everything. I smiled back and could at least see they were happy for me.

I sat back while the conversation flowed around me. Different people filled Kathleen and me in on what had been happening over the last few days. I felt a pang for missing the fun, but would not trade running into Padraig and spending time with him for anything. Anne finally came back, noticeably calmer, but still with no ETA for our parents' arrival. We hung out a little longer and then people started parting ways for the evening. It was a small town and we were all staying in the same place, so we were sure to see each other, no matter what.

Anne, Kathleen, Padraig, and I walked back to the hotel together. James and his friends had gone off, but promised to find Padraig before too long to "save him from the girls." It was nice to have some quiet time with just us to really relax and let Padraig settle in a bit more. We made ourselves comfortable in the common room.

"*So,* Padraig."

Uh-oh. Here we go. I should have known we wouldn't get off that easy. I looked at Anne, who sat on a couch opposite the one where Padraig and I had settled. Kathleen was in a loveseat perpendicular to the two couches and looked back and forth as if she were watching a tennis match.

"One week you've known my sister," she pressed on. "That's not a long time. You seem quite taken—as of course you should be—but what exactly are your intentions, sir?"

Anne was always protective, being six whole minutes older than me, but seriously? I raised an eyebrow as I felt Padraig stiffen next to me. Kathleen snorted as she tried to hold in a laugh. She'd seen Anne's mouth twitching. How had I missed that? We broke up, lost in fits of laughter, though Padraig's may have been a bit more forced than ours.

"I'm totally kidding!" Anne finally managed.

Poor guy. Oh, what he was in for, especially once he met Dad. Good thing our father was off on an errand so we could ease into this. Anne's ice breaker led to more idle chatter. Stories from growing up, stories from college. Eventually Kathleen and I exchanged a glance; it was time to break for showers and start the evening's festivities. Someone must have tipped James off too, because he came in then and told Anne he was taking her to dinner and she needed to shower and change.

Kathleen and I called the others to set the plan in motion, then got ready ourselves. Padraig had somehow been absorbed into the group by James and his groomsmen and was staying in one of their rooms, which he seemed just fine with, thank goodness. Luckily, everything was happening so fast, I really didn't have time to stop and think how quick—and maybe even a little strange—this was. Tomorrow? Shoot, I was having trouble keeping up with today.

At six o'clock, the girls were gathered in front of the hotel and ready for the evening. Marie had brought a beauty queen sash that read BACHELORETTE across it, which Michelle took one look at and said, "Oh, lord!" I *knew* this would be a great evening. My gift was a plastic shot glass on a string of beads to hang around her neck. As the others planned how to make Anne wear these, I went upstairs to get the guest of honor. As I passed the common room, I caught Padraig's gaze. He was talking with one of the groomsmen. He acknowledged me with a nod and walked over.

"My offer still stands—to be a chaperone and all. I think I might rather like seeing you out on the piss with your sister."

"Well ... legends have been made, stories told."

He laughed and leaned forward to give me a light kiss on the lips. "Something to remember me by."

As if I needed anything. I smiled up at him as the butterflies fluttered all around my stomach (oh, how I had missed those), and then continued up the stairs. I arrived at my sister's door just as James was knocking. He winked at me as she answered, looking back and forth at us in confusion.

"Hi," I said. "Turn around, and don't ask any questions." She gave me a look, but did as she was told. I tied the blindfold around her head, and James gave her a quick kiss.

"Have fun," he said, as I guided her down the hallway.

I tried to keep my sister from bumping into things, though it took all my willpower. Maybe I was enjoying this just a tad too much. As we walked out the front door to join the girls, I heard Padraig yell his own, "Have fun!"

We did just that.

# 27

I opened an eye and saw nothing but carpet. Hmm ... how had that happened? I tried to turn my head to look around for more clues, and got a beam of sunlight in the eye. *Ouch*. Bright.

I heard a slight moan from near my feet and glanced down to see what I thought was the side of Kathleen's head. Whoever it was, she had a pillow. Nice. I moved a bit more and realized I had a blanket on me. Well, at least that was something.

I laid for a bit more, dozing off and on, and then decided I could sit up. Just a bit though, and slowly. I smelled coffee. That helped.

Once in the upright position, I realized I was sitting next to a bed with a familiar comforter. Oh good, so Kathleen and I had made it back to our room. Then the bed moved, and I was looking into eyes identical to my own.

"Good morning, bachelorette. You're in my bed."

Another moan was all I got in response. Well, I guess we pretty much resembled zombies. I looked to my other side and noticed a much bigger lump, then two pairs of feet. Michelle and Marie? We girls knew how to party *and* stick together. I thought I heard a creak and looked to see that someone had slipped packets of ibuprofen under the door.

Cute.

But I'd take it.

Now, water ...

For some reason, the thought of water made me think of Jameson. That was not a good thing. The Jameson had been free-flowing last night, and I'd found out personally that one could definitely have too much of a good thing.

I was able to take small sips of water and the ibuprofen went down no problem. Things were looking up already. I washed my face and brushed my teeth, then threw on some clothes and ventured down the hallway to find the dining room. A light-filled room with floor-to-ceiling glass walls and chattering, nicely dressed people greeted me. Oh, boy—too much.

Luckily, none of the boys were among them. They must have had about as much fun as we had, at least it looked like it the last time I'd seen them. I quickly (as quickly as possible anyway) loaded a tray with mugs of tea, coffee, and toast to take back to the room, then made a hasty exit before any more curious glances came my way.

The girls were stirring when I got back and grateful for the gifts I was bearing. I noticed little pill packets ripped open and lying about. So they had started the morning as I had. The bachelorette was now sitting up and looking a little more with it, so I handed her a mug of tea. She took a sip. "Did Marie really sing to me while sitting on the bar last night?" We heard a moan from across the room, and I grinned.

"I would take that as a yes," I replied and turned to see Marie with her head buried in her pillow. "What song was it? I forget."

"I believe that would be 'Like a G-6'," Michelle answered and started singing.

"Gawd, I hate that song too" Marie said, and then laughed.

Kathleen came out of the bathroom, looking better than the rest of us, being freshly showered and dressed. Yes, that would definitely help. She had also laid off the whiskey earlier than we had. Smart girl.

There was a knock on the door, and Kathleen opened it to find James standing on the other side. He was looking a bit the worse for wear as well. He glanced in and his eyes found Anne.

"Ah, here you are. How is everyone? I have a bunch of sleeping bums in my room right now."

Anne managed a weak smile, then slowly stood up and walked over to give her soon-to-be groom a good morning hug. They spoke briefly and she turned with a small wave, saying she'd see us later. Probably off to take a hot shower.

Michelle and Marie started gathering themselves as well, then went off to their own room to get ready for the day. I realized I had no idea what time it was and glanced over at the alarm clock. Nine in the morning. Wow, my latest start all trip! Amazing. I found myself wondering if Padraig had already been up for hours or if the late night had dragged him down as well. I showered quickly (which helped), then dressed so Kathleen and I could head out for a more substantial breakfast.

We found the dining room still open and thankfully only occupied by our friends, all looking like we felt. I scanned the room until I found Padraig, sitting between two groomsmen and smiling at me. He seemed amused, either at something one of the guys had said or at Kathleen and me shuffling in with stifled yawns. I felt Kathleen straighten up and followed her line of sight to Cian sitting at a table as well.

People had food in front of them, so we found a table and sat. I took a glance at the menu, though eggs sounded perfect to me. I smelled pancakes, which started to sound good too, but Kathleen and I stuck with the eggs and ordered Irish Breakfasts. This would be one of the last chances, after all. At least for me, I thought soberly. Kathleen was going to live here! I still hadn't quite wrapped my head around that.

"Hey, Kathleen!" a voice yelled from across the room. "Nice vocals last night!"

Kathleen stared at me in horror. I stared back blankly. She'd *sung*? A fuzzy memory started coming back to me, and I burst out laughing.

She finally found her voice and turned to look at Cian. "I sang last night?"

He grinned at her. "Yes, love. You did. I was quite proud too. You sounded pretty good!"

"That's *right*," I said. "I remember now—someone talked Cian into singing at O'Connor's and you decided to get up and do a duet. What did you guys sing—?"

"'Danny Boy'," Gerry supplied, with a laugh.

"Seriously?" Kathleen seemed to remember and shook her head. "Were we trying to bring the place down?"

"It was classic," Padraig piped in, and James nodded in agreement.

Padraig had been there too? When had the boys joined us? The bachelors already had their night. More fuzzy memories started coming in. I guess in a small town it was only a matter of time before people's paths would cross.

Our breakfasts came out, and we went silent as we started in. It was nice to finally be hungry, but I still went slowly. I took a pause and glanced over at Padraig to check in with him. He was in an animated conversation with James, which made me happy. He was mixing with everyone so easily. Definitely not something I was used to from my last relationship. I went back to my food, and a short while later Kathleen and I both sat back from our plates. It was good to have a full stomach, and now more sleep seemed like a good idea.

"Hey, sis."

Anne had dropped into a seat next to mine, and I hadn't even noticed. I *really* needed more sleep.

"A bunch of us are talking about driving to the Cliffs of Moher in a bit. Maybe the fresh air will help our heads. Want to come?"

I just stared at her. That sounded so—active. She gave me a small knowing smile, probably able to read me pretty well.

"Padraig mentioned being fine staying here and seeing a little more of Doolin, so if you're thinking that sounds like a lot, maybe he could use a tour guide." She glanced over at Kathleen. "Cian said he'd go, hasn't visited since he was young."

Well then. That settled it. Kathleen got up to find Cian and start making plans, and I started clearing our plates.

"Parking can be tricky now with all the tour buses, so this way we can take fewer cars," Anne said as she helped. I gave her a grateful smile, and she winked back. "Ah, here comes your charge now."

I looked up to see Padraig working his way among the tables to join us. Even in my foggy state, my heart did a little jump. Boy, was this fun. I would try and keep the darkness that was starting to enter at bay. Tomorrow was the wedding, and then leaving soon after ...

"So, looks like it's you and me, kid," he said, with a smile.

I think I gave him a shameless smile in return, though I held in the sigh. He leaned in close to help clear some plates and his hip brushed against mine. Okay, *now* I was starting to wake up. Anne left us to it and moved to join the others who had gathered to make the plan for the day. The cliffs were breathtaking and I felt a pang at missing them, but I could not pass up this extra time with Padraig. As it was, the time we had was short and my growing fantasy probably unrealistic, but if we were to have any chance ...

We finished up on autopilot (a team efficiency developed from our work at Keldun House?) and left the dining room. Since I had some energy, I suggested we walk around town for a while. The air would definitely help, and then I could come back and fall on my face (though I did not want to give up too much time with Padraig). He agreed and we followed the others towards the front door, waving them off and then starting our stroll down Fisher Street.

He took my hand, a gesture becoming more and more familiar (yet still exciting!), and we peeked into shops here and there. At one point I stopped to admire a picture in a window and he put his arms around me, giving me a hug from behind. I caught a glimpse of us in the reflection and thought I might burst from happiness. Cheesy, I know, but I couldn't help it. Again, I had to mentally pinch myself to realize this was really happening. Crazy, but I was determined to just stop thinking and enjoy it.

I was too charmed by a pink, thatched cottage not to go in, so I talked Padraig into doing some browsing with me. I moved around the room admiring the wares, and he chatted with the shop owner. I found myself admiring him as well and kept having to refocus. I had this urge to commemorate the moment, and the trip in general, and bought myself a cozy brown sweater. I tried to tell myself it was *not* to match the one I had so admired on Padraig.

We also stopped into a music shop where I bought some CDs and Padraig practiced playing a guitar. (He had some experience and was actually pretty good!) When we wandered into a shop with lots of local crafts and trinkets, I again found myself gazing at Padraig as he moved around, holding things up here and there to show me. I especially liked the mug saying "Póg Mo Thóin"—that he said he'd once bought for his brother—and had to stifle a giggle, remembering the shot glass I'd bought for Anne and James.

I had entirely too much fun and walked out with a bag full of jams and soaps and candles. Padraig was carrying a bag too, which was curious because I hadn't known he was looking for anything. I hadn't even seen him at the register. He just smiled at me, and we continued walking. My stomach growled (how embarrassing!) and Padraig laughed.

"Hungry, I take it?"

I laughed too, sure that my cheeks were turning horribly pink.

"I'm feeling it a bit too," he continued, "and it *is* lunchtime. Want to stop for a bite to eat? The others won't be back for a while yet."

I agreed, and we found ourselves back at O'Connor's. I grabbed a table, and he went to the bar for drinks and a menu. We were already developing a routine. He came back with Bulmers for me, Guinness for himself. We sipped our drinks and glanced at the menu, deciding on soup and bread. Padraig went to place our order and returned looking somewhat serious. He took my hand across the table and my heart dropped. I had no idea what he might have in mind.

"Amelia, meeting you and spending time together has been fantastic," he said. "What else can I say, but that I want it to continue? I'm not going to beat around the bush ... I like you very much, and I think we really have something. There. I said it."

Padraig sat back and released a breath. I sat in shock. Of course, this was what I wanted to hear, and my heart was doing wild cartwheels, but I certainly had not expected it. He was watching me expectantly and I could sense his nervousness, so I tried to get my brain to come up with something to say. I managed a stunned smile (very attractive, surely), then found my voice.

"I'm glad you said that, Padraig, because I'm not sure I would have had the nerve. I totally agree," I said, giving his hand a squeeze. "These last few days have been amazing and definitely the best I've felt, well, maybe ever."

"Well, good," he replied, a big smile on his face—mixed with relief. "Then I can give you this."

He reached into his shopping bag and pulled out a small package wrapped in tissue paper. He handed it across the table and sat back.

"I hope you like it. Something to remember me by." He winked and gestured for me to open it.

I tried not to fumble too much as I worked the tissue paper with nervous hands. The anticipation, the excitement, his expectant look ... it all flashed through my mind at once. I finally revealed a small box with a silver necklace nestled inside—a solid, heart-shaped pendant on a delicate chain, with Celtic knot designs making up the center. It was so beautiful and so perfect. I really did not know what to say. I finally looked up and my eyes met his.

"Well ... do you like it?"

"I ... love it," I managed, still a little stunned and probably not saying the right thing at all. A lot had happened in the last few minutes. "Thank you."

He continued to hold my gaze and I thought I saw a glint of humor in his. "Don't worry; it doesn't mean we're engaged or anything. I just wanted you to have it."

I giggled at the line from *Aliens* (did he really know one of my favorite movies?) and felt a bit of the tension break. "So you're not giving me your heart then?" I asked playfully.

"Well—" Now it was his turn to be uncomfortable.

"I'm just kidding." I rushed in to save him, feeling on sure footing again. "It's beautiful. Thank you very much." I fumbled with the clasp and managed to hook it around my neck. "So this was in your bag of mystery. I didn't even see you shopping."

"I am a man of mystery, yes. Actually, I bought something else too." He reached into his bag again and pulled out a watercolor painting. "I didn't want to show up at the wedding empty-handed. Do you think Anne and James will like it?"

I studied it closer and saw a charming scene of life in Doolin. "Oh, look at that. What a perfect way to remember their time here. They'll love it! How thoughtful." I was really starting to think this guy was one-in-a-million.

Our food came just then, so we put our conversation on hold and dug in. As I sipped soup from my spoon, I absently fingered my new necklace and started to feel a warm glow. On the inside from the soup, on the outside from happiness—again with the cheesy—but I couldn't help it. Perhaps I had sensed this in him, making the feelings I was having not so crazy after all.

We finally sat back. Padraig took a swig of Guinness and I munched brown bread. "The others should be getting back soon," he said. "Should we start heading back?"

I wanted to keep sitting there with him, but I also wanted to connect with Anne and jump into wedding plans. "I guess we should. You can relax some more, and I can start being a proper maid of honor."

We paid our tab at the bar, then walked back onto the street. Padraig took my hand (I would *not* think about the dwindling number of days I had left of this). Before we knew it, we were back at Cullinan's and stopped outside the front door. Padraig looked like he wanted to say something, but then we heard a commotion behind us and turned to see the rest of our group hopping out of cars and coming to join us. Kathleen was the first to reach us, all pink-cheeked from the cold.

"That was great! You guys missed a beautiful day out there." She turned to me, and I saw her eyes shift briefly to my throat. "Did you have fun, though?"

"Yes, we did," I answered and held up my shopping bags. "We had a nice lunch too."

"Lunch! Oh man, I'm starving." With that, she was off.

The rest of the group moved past us, all talking about lunch as well. Anne and James were the last, and Anne side-eyed me as she walked by with a small smile but said nothing. Then it was just me and Padraig again.

He looked down at me with an unreadable expression on his face. "I've been wanting to do this all day," was all he said before leaning down and planting a kiss. I was surprised, but found my hands unconsciously reaching out to rest at his hips, which he seemed to take as encouragement, because the kiss deepened.

In the back of my mind, I was wondering if anyone was around and noticing, but I also found I didn't really care. I felt like every nerve in my body was awake and perhaps even singing. This crazy, cute Irishman who had come out of the blue! Did things like this really happen and actually work out? Oh, I hoped so, because I did not want this to end.

We finally came up for air and stood grinning at each other, probably stupidly. I put my hand on his arm and turned to lead him through the doorway, trying to calm my racing heart at the same time. As we started down the hall, he said, "I think last night is catching up with me. See you later on for dinner?" I could actually picture my pillow quite easily and agreed. He gave me a soft peck and continued on to the room where he was staying.

I think I stood for a moment with my heart fluttering, just staring. What a cheesewad.

I shook myself and headed into my room. Kathleen looked up, seeming rather happy herself.

"How was your time?" she asked as I kicked off my shoes and flopped onto my bed.

"So great! I'm wiped out, though. All I want is a nap."

"You haven't slept yet?" she asked, as she sat on my bed.

"People always say being in love gives you a crazy amount of energy." Had I just said *in love*?

She bugged her eyes out at me and then laughed—though she didn't look surprised.

"I think we decided to date long-distance," I continued.

My friend just shook her head and smiled at me. "Well, that's the best thing I've heard in a long time. Besides Anne and James getting married, I guess." Now the giggles set in as the events of the last few days really sank in on us. Who knew what life could do?

"I haven't really told Anne about all this," I said, when we settled down. "I guess I should, huh."

"Oh, don't worry. Anne and I have been talking. I've filled her in," Kathleen informed me. "Besides, she could see it all over you. How could she not?"

I felt myself blush. So, I hadn't been as cool and collected as I imagined. Oh well. I hadn't scared Padraig away, so that was good.

"And have you decided for sure about staying here with the band?" I figured she was and had felt her making the transition already, but had to ask. Not pulling away exactly, just seeming more solid in this place. She was definitely happier than I'd seen her in a long time, and there was a different spark in her.

"Yeah, I have." She smiled, and it was so peaceful I could only smile back. "I don't know what will happen with Cian, but that feels good too. I need to make this change. It's actually all set—I've been waiting to tell you. Out at the cliffs I called my principal, and we had a good talk. They'll combine classrooms, no one loses a job. Quite smooth, actually."

"I'm so happy for you," was all I could think to say as I leaned over and gave her a hug. Guess all my nudges had worked. Maybe too well? I would miss my friend, but we were going to have some really good phone conversations.

"Okay, now I'm closing my eyes before Anne comes and wants to do wedding stuff. Wake me in an hour, if I'm not already?"

"Will do," Kathleen replied, and snapped off a mock salute.

My head hit the pillow, I sighed in contentment, and drifted off to sleep with a small smile on my face.

# 28

The big day dawned bright and beautiful. After the rains and storms of the past few days, not even a cloud in the sky. Thank gawd. Some of the party couldn't believe it was here. I was one of them.

With memories of the previous day with Padraig, I pulled myself out of bed to start getting ready. There were hours yet before the ceremony, but Anne would be excited and frantic and wanting me at her side for whatever might come. Most of the unfinished details—like hand-tying little white satin ribbons on the dark green, engraved tealight holders they were giving as wedding favors—had been taken care of the day before, but who knew what could pop up. We'd also made the official introduction of Padraig to my parents.

I smiled again, remembering. There'd been the expected amount of speculation from their side (mostly my dad) and proper, positive-impression efforts from Padraig's side. A solid handshake from Dad, a warm hug and I-want-to-hear-all-about-this-later look from Mom. It was quicker than I had hoped, with all the little tasks to be tended to, but it may also have been for the best. I had sensed some tension between the two, definitely uneasy looks from Mom directed towards Dad. For people who had been divorced for many years they got on remarkably well, but still—there were moments.

I went over the morning schedule in my head. We wanted to get to the church in Lisdoonvarna with plenty of time for pictures and set-up and, with the way this trip had gone, I was not taking any chances. A lot could happen trying to move a group of people nine miles.

Kathleen was still sleeping, so I tried to move through the bathroom as quickly and quietly as possible, all the while thinking of Padraig and my nearing departure. A little sadness crept in around the edges, making me feel guilty for being so preoccupied with my own thoughts on such an important day for my sister, but I just couldn't help it. It seemed like things didn't bother happening when it was convenient.

I showered quickly, knowing most of the preparation would happen at the church. Makeup, dresses—all would be easier there (and more fun) and no one would have to worry about a wrinkled dress. I noted the time and figured I'd give Kathleen another thirty minutes. If I didn't see her at breakfast, I'd come back up and give her a shake.

The breakfast room was abuzz with energy and excitement. The bride and groom were looking rather relaxed, which was a good sign. All must be going smoothly for the moment. Mom sat with Michelle and Marie, enjoying toast and coffee, while Dad chatted with some of the groomsmen. Padraig glanced up from a table at the far corner of the room where he was pouring a mug of coffee for himself. My heart jumped a bit at his smile—would I always react like this?—and I made my way over to greet him and grab a mug of tea. I knew this was my sister's day, but I couldn't resist the pull, and she was occupied with her groom. Just a quick "Good morning" to him, and I'd join her. I needed to make the most of my time left, after all, though I didn't want to focus too much on it.

Knowing any eyes could be on us, including my parents', we shared a very quick, very chaste peck on the lips. He handed me a mug with a murmured "G'morning" and gave me a small grin. "Sleep well?"

"Yes. You?" Unfortunately it had been alone, but we both understood it had to be this way—for now. It was enough to know the wanting was on both sides, and I had to have a little faith that things would work out as they were meant to.

His eyes tracked over my shoulder, and I turned to see my sister approaching, Kathleen in tow. Good, I didn't have to wake her up.

"Hello, young lovers! Enough of that. Today is my day, and it's time to get it going."

She grabbed my hand and pulled me, along with Kathleen, towards a nearby table. "You can come too," she threw over her shoulder to Padraig. "This wedding group needs to get fortified and then move out!"

He obliged, with a laugh, and we all sat down to enjoy another breakfast feast. We really did need to set our foundation now, because who knew when we'd be eating again once the day really took off. Perhaps not until the reception later that afternoon. Everyone tucked into their eggs, potatoes, baked beans, tomatoes, pancakes, French toast, oatmeal—anything we could want, it was here. I was determined to enjoy every last bit.

The morning went by in a blur. Hours later I stood with arms crossed, watching Anne and James take photos and finally drew a deep breath. I stood next to the gorgeous stone cathedral Anne had booked for the ceremony and reception. Technically called a church—Corpus Christi Church—but one of the most beautiful and ancient I had ever seen. Apparently James' ancestors had attended it and the secondary school next door. It had meant a lot to him to get married here, and I could see why. I thought how beautiful their pictures would be, the way the lowering light hit the stone and cast intriguing shadows across the walls.

A movement out of the corner of my eye made me turn. Kathleen came hurrying towards me, though with a smile. It was nice seeing my friend so happy after what she had confessed to me during the trip. She looked beautiful in her bridesmaid dress. Anne had chosen a deep sage, sheath-style, and it complimented all of us. I looked down at myself, thinking I looked pretty good as well.

"Are you ready?" she asked me, all excitement and energy. I had a feeling it had a little to do with Cian and not just the pace of the day. "They're almost done with pictures. We need to get the shots ready."

Ah yes! We had a little surprise for Anne, to help steady the nerves. I nodded and followed her, ready to officially start the ceremony.

We were putting the last of the glasses of Jameson on a shiny tray we'd found in the church kitchen when Anne walked in with our mom following. From the looks they kept sharing, it seemed they'd been having a nice heart-to-heart.

Mom had been in full support of our Jameson plan, knowing Anne might need some calming of the nerves today. Mom was usually right and from the look on Anne's face, today was no exception.

Anne still looked fairly good, but I could tell the energy was starting to build. Her eyes found mine, and she walked right towards me and grabbed my wrists.

"This is really happening!"

"Yes, and it's about time!" I gave her a hug, careful not to wrinkle her dress.

Her eyes looked down at the tray I'd just loaded.

"We thought we could all use a little toast to properly commence with this event. I only poured a little bit," I hurried to assure her. We loved our Jameson.

She took a deep breath and looked around the room, smiling at all of us—Michelle, Marie, Kathleen, me, Mom.

"I really can't believe this, you guys. All of us—here—in Ireland. This day ..."

Her eyes started to glisten, and I took it as a good time to circulate the shots. I grabbed the tray and made sure everyone had a glass in hand. Taking a deep breath, I raised my own.

"To my sister, the most beautiful bride."

I saw tears threatening again but pushed on.

"Here's to finding your match and bringing us all to this beautiful place to make it official. I couldn't picture it happening anywhere else, surrounded by anyone else."

I raised my glass and everyone ended with "Sláinte!" and took their sips. Just a bit to warm the insides and steel the nerves. We shared smiles all around and made our way out to take our places.

The ceremony went off without a hitch. Anne and James were radiant, with eyes only for each other. No one passed out walking down the aisle (though we had joked about it), maybe thanks to the shot of whiskey. I thought Anne actually might, when I hiked up my dress and climbed onto a table to give my speech at the reception, as I'd threatened to do when we read about the Celtic tradition. I didn't break my glass as was traditional though—to everyone's relief—just shot back the whiskey with the rest of the room.

I also thought *I* might faint when Padraig held out his hand and asked me to dance. "But Cora said she couldn't get you to dance," I said.

He simply smiled and took me into his arms as some lovely Irish aire played, whirling us around the floor and literally taking my breath away. Cian was also quite the dancer, which was perfect for Kathleen, though I'm sure she wouldn't have minded if he weren't. When she wasn't gazing up at him on stage, they were tearing up the dance floor.

Anne and James were in their own blissful world, as they should have been, though she did break away long enough to share one of our favorite songs with me. Cian and the boys played "Closing Time" by Semisonic, and we sang along as we danced. There's a line in the song mentioning a new beginning coming from a beginning's end, which we both loved. She gave me a special smile and I smiled back, thinking of all the changes that had happened recently. The new job, time with Kathleen, meeting Padraig. Amazing what life could bring.

Padraig was able to grab some time to present them with the painting he'd bought. James was touched and gave him a manly hug and Anne had tears in her eyes, though it may have had less to do with the gift and more to do with why she kept grinning at me. Sisters.

Before we knew it, the night was wrapping up and it was time for everyone to make their way back to Doolin. The car service dropped us off in time for one more drink. We agreed on McGann's, made the short trip to the pub, and ordered pints. The group was getting tired. We'd celebrated the afternoon and night to the fullest, but no one wanted to say good night just yet.

I took the opportunity to find a quiet spot with Padraig, wanting to enjoy every last moment with him. I tried not to be dramatic or think on it too heavily, but it was hard. Our time was quickly coming to a close.

I had so much to say, and it seemed he did too, but we sat close together just enjoying the live music that had started and relaxing. This just felt so—*normal*. Could our long distance attempt work out? I vowed in that moment that it would. I would do all I could to make it so.

A warm hand gripped mine and squeezed, as if in understanding. I looked into Padraig's eyes and leaned in a little closer, determined not to think of the morning. For tonight, the familiar sounds of the jigs and reels would work to soothe my nerves, and Padraig's, too, it seemed. We settled into the music and each other, enjoying watching the rest of our party from afar and hearing their murmured conversations.

All too soon, the bartender was calling last call and musicians were on their way out the door. I felt bad not spending more time with Anne and the rest of the group, but everyone had seemed content to just get pulled into the music and make small talk here and there. They also understood us wanting to spend these final moments together, and I'd even seen a few glances sent our way. Mostly glad at seeing me find this great guy and unexpected happiness, but also sympathetic to the hardship of the situation.

We all walked through the quiet streets of Doolin back to the B&B and exchanged quick hugs and good nights. Then it was just Padraig and me, left in the lobby to share one more hug and kiss. I was determined to make the most of the moment and not get pulled too quickly into the thoughts and sadness of leaving.

Trying to ride on the energy and fun of the day, I walked to him slowly and twined my arms up and around his neck. "Something to remember me by," I said, with a grin, as I pulled his head down towards mine. His lips curved into an appreciative smile as he cupped the back of my head, bringing us even closer and squeezing me tight against him for a deep kiss. We stayed that way for I don't know how long, enjoying each other in the quiet lobby.

A clock somewhere near us chimed midnight, and we figured we should get some sleep before our departure in just a few hours. Padraig walked me to my room like a proper gentleman, and after one more kiss, left me outside my door.

# 29

Morning came and everyone went their way. Anne and James to start their honeymoon; Cian and the boys to another gig; some guests to fly out of Shannon airport; and Kathleen, Padraig, and me to drive back to Dublin. At least I hadn't had to say goodbye to him just yet, though that was fast approaching.

I thought back to our conversation when he gave me the necklace and how refreshing it was; how sure and straightforward he had been. Then, I started wondering if he also wanted me to stay in Ireland. He hadn't come out and said it, only that he wanted to see where we could go. From two different continents, that could be pretty difficult. Was I crazy to fly back now? Kathleen was staying. Could I drop everything and do the same?

At the moment I couldn't imagine that, having worked so hard to finally get into my career, but weren't people more important? And careers weren't much without someone to share them with. Of course, there was no guarantee things would work out with Padraig and then where would I be? I had gone down that road once already, living in a place for a guy and being even more devastated when it ended and having no one to turn to or any real reason to be there. Picking up and moving on from that—it just seemed to be extra painful.

Oh, my brain. I wondered if anyone could hear the wheels furiously turning, but Padraig and Kathleen were deep in conversation with memories of the wedding. Although I figured Kathleen was excited about her new direction, I wondered if Padraig was having any thoughts similar to mine. As I tried to relax and look at the scenery passing by outside, I tuned into our road trip CD. Enya was singing "Only Time." Not a big help.

All too soon we were pulling into the rental office to return the car, after a quick stop at the B&B to drop luggage and take it to the room we'd reserved for our return. The place was empty, so we were in and out in no time and walking back towards Baggot Court. Padraig still had the day off so headed to his place to change, saying he would meet us later in Temple Bar for the evening.

I really could not wrap my brain around the fact that I was leaving the next day and would not see him for a while. He'd made such a place in my life in so short a time. Kathleen must have sensed this, because she linked her arm in mine and gave me a little squeeze.

We climbed the steps to Baggot Court and seemed to have the same idea at the same moment. "Wine?" I asked.

"Wine," she replied.

I motioned her down the hallway towards the outdoor garden area and ran upstairs to get the bottle we had bought earlier in the trip and two glasses. When I rejoined my friend, I was finally able to say what had been slowly entering my heart.

"I'm having second thoughts," I said. "About leaving tomorrow." She would know what I meant and maybe not be surprised. We knew each other that well.

Kathleen nodded quietly and seemed thoughtful as she poured our wine and handed me a glass. We gave each other a little salute, then took a sip.

"I'm sure you are," she said, eyeing me closely. "You *can* stay, y'know. We've always talked of living here together, and I'm sure you could connect to a publishing house over here."

I slowly shook my head. "That's just so impulsive," I countered. "I mean, you were unhappy with your situation, but I'm not. I've finally reached where I want to be, and this thing with Padraig just happened. How can I justify such a knee-jerk reaction?"

"I know you were a bit hasty last time, but you were happy. It didn't work out, but what if it had? You would do it again, wouldn't you?"

"Yeah, I probably would. I just want to be smarter this time, and if it's right it'll work out, right? People do long distance all the time. That's what airplanes are for."

"Do you get to travel a lot as an editor? Maybe discover an Irish author and need to come here for official meetings?"

I loved that she was trying to make me feel better, whatever I chose to do. I took another sip and looked around at the array of bright flowers in bold blue pots surrounding us and creating a border for the small stone patio. Even they seemed to be trying to make me feel better.

I think what I really needed was a night of whiskey and fun—and to stop thinking so much. We finished our wine, corked the bottle for Kathleen to enjoy later, and headed upstairs to change for the evening.

We decided on The Quays, where it had all started. The three of us grabbed dinner on the upper level and then made our way downstairs to enjoy music. We found a table with familiar smiling faces. Cora, David, Liam, and Seamus sat waiting. Padraig had planned the surprise for us.

Cora slid over for me and Kathleen to join her so we could share all we had been up to. She wanted to hear all about the wedding and how Padraig had come to join us. I couldn't resist telling her about the dance, and she raised her eyebrows but only said "Can't say I'm all that surprised," which made me curious.

As Padraig was involved with the guys, I decided to mention Gwynn as well. Cora raised her eyebrows again and gave me a thoughtful look. She shook her head and laughed. "Well, I'm sure it's nothing to worry about. At least on Padraig's end."

"So, there *is* something." Now the hairs on the back of my neck were starting to stand.

"Maybe I'll tell you a bit more one day," she replied, patting my hand. "For now, just enjoy the evening and Padraig. Don't end your time on a worry."

I liked that and would try. It was nice to talk with her, and we eventually sat back and marveled at all that had happened. Cian entering into the equation; Kathleen's change of heart and decision to stay. It was hard to be melancholy when listening to Kathleen's excitement, and I enjoyed getting caught up in her lively retelling to Cora.

My focus kept landing on Padraig, and I found myself wanting to be alone with him. Every so often our eyes would connect, and I wondered what he was thinking. He kept giving me that wonderful smile of his. I found myself getting caught up in conversation around the table, which helped. I wanted to enjoy my last night in Ireland and the ending of an incredible trip. We made toasts to old friends and new friends, to crazy adventures, and new beginnings.

Soon enough, Cora shoved us off the bench to dance, and Seamus joined the band with his bodhrán. No falling off the stage this time, much to everyone's disappointment. The only excitement came when Padraig asked me for another dance. I loved the shocked and delighted faces, but soon forgot them as he pulled me close and we swayed together. He even sang a bit in my ear. What, I can't exactly remember. What I do remember is that he had a lovely bass voice, and I could get very used to hearing it.

Again the pull to stay was very strong, but I needed to take a deep breath and be smart about it. I would love to get caught up and follow my heart, but my head knew I needed to complete this part of the journey and reassess from a distance. Things had a way of working out, right?

Back at the table, we were received with catcalls and whistles. David playfully punched Padraig in the arm, and Cora squeezed my knee.

"Is no one really going to talk about this? You two are adorable—and we got to see it happen! Are you really leaving tomorrow?"

I felt my pulse quicken as she voiced what I had been thinking about. Everyone was staring at me. Padraig rushed to the rescue. "We'll figure it out," he said. "Amelia has obligations." But I was touched that they cared enough to get involved.

"I could only get so much time off, and it's a new job so I don't want to push it," I explained.

"Ah, come on!" Liam chimed in. No girls were drawing his attention, so he'd stayed with us and the conversation. "Jobs come and go. This is love! She's staying." He turned to Kathleen. "C'mon, talk some sense into her."

Kathleen laughed and held up her hands. "Our situations are different. She's doing what she needs to."

"And chivalry isn't dead," David was quick to add. "Maybe Padraig will just have to hop on a plane and visit her in San Francisco."

I liked the sound of that! I smiled at him gratefully, and he saluted me with his glass in return.

"Alright, everyone," Padraig cut in. "A final toast before we all call it a night." We raised our shots of whiskey and looked at him expectantly. "Here's to this one life we get, and doing the best with it that we can." We said a collective "Sláinte!" and finished our glasses. I stole another glance at Padraig and found him looking at me as well. He gave me a wink, and I smiled back.

We stood up to leave. Since I had already exchanged contact information with Cora, we simply hugged and promised to write soon. She wished me a safe flight, with an extra pat on the back and a knowing look. We all made our way outside with the other pub-goers and spilled onto the cobblestoned streets of Temple Bar. One more goodbye and we took our different directions home, Padraig joining Kathleen and me.

The walk seemed to take no time, no matter how much I tried to slow it down and drink in every detail. It was starting to sink in that I would be leaving not only Padraig tomorrow, but Kathleen as well. Was I really ready for this? At the door to Baggot Court, Kathleen left me and Padraig to say goodbye in private. Without a word, he pulled me into him and held me close. The warmth and shelter of his arms was becoming my favorite place in the world.

"You don't have to go, y'know. I wouldn't mind if you stayed."

I pulled back and looked into his smile. How could this all be happening so fast? And why couldn't he have said that two days ago when I could have wrapped my brain more around it?

"I certainly don't want to, but it's so fast. I really do have to get back to work ..." I trailed off, feeling how lame that sounded.

He stepped back and held my hands, holding them between us. "I know, and it's easier for me. David's right. It's a two-way street. We'll figure it out." He gave me a smile, though it seemed to waver a little. "I wish I could come up or we could go somewhere together, but I guess I should let you get your rest now. And Kathleen will be waiting."

"Yeah, I guess." I couldn't even try to sound convincing. Maybe not being too intimate would make leaving tomorrow a bit easier. And the reunion (if it was meant) that much stronger. "I know you have to work tomorrow, so it's totally fine if you don't come to the airport. Probably better ... This goodbye is hard enough."

"Well, I'll see you in the morning anyway. This isn't it." He gave me another smile, then put his hands on either side of my face and pulled me in for one last kiss. This one was gentle but had more urgency than the others. It deepened for a bit and we clung to each other before he pulled back, and we stood looking at each other. He pulled me to him once more, gave a little squeeze, and then released me.

"See you in the morning. Have a good sleep." With that, he turned and walked down the street.

I stared after him a moment, then went inside and made my way upstairs, feeling like weights were tied to my hands and feet. Kathleen looked up expectantly when I walked in and crossed the room to give me a hug. To my credit, I held the tears back. They came when the lights were out.

# 30

I woke early and was ready in record time. I was trying to stay calm and just prepare for getting back home and rejoining life in San Francisco, but I also needed to see Padraig. Kathleen helped me lug my bag down the stairs and we entered the lobby. There was Padraig at the counter, just as I had first seen him a week ago. He glanced up and gave me that smile, and I melted. Despite my inner conflict, seeing him made me feel better.

He stepped away from the desk and gave me a good morning hug. Kathleen tried to avert her eyes to give us privacy for our last moments together and even went into the dining room to get me some breakfast for the road.

Since he was at work and with guests around, we only had a brief time to say another goodbye, which was fine with me. Any more drawn out and I would have crumpled altogether. We shared another hug and a more chaste kiss, then Kathleen and I dragged my bag out the door to the cab awaiting us at the curb. I couldn't think any more on the finality of my ending, so turned the conversation to Kathleen on the drive to the airport.

"Thanks for coming out to see me off," I said. "What's first on the list for you?"

"It should be housing, which I'm honestly not sure about just yet. Cian said he has some connections, though, and since this is the beginning of their tour we're basically hitting the road right away. I'm excited to get caught up in what's already been planned and start figuring my role as we go."

"Sounds fabulous. You'll have to tell me about it, every step of the way." It really was nice getting caught up in her excitement.

"I will. We'll talk all the time. And Am?"

I turned to look at her questioningly.

"I get why you're doing it. Going, I mean. You guys will figure it out, and he's a good one. You can be sure of him."

I gave her a grateful smile. I had needed to hear that more than I realized. She patted my arm and turned to look out the window as we got closer and closer to the airport. Soon we were pulling over to the curb and jumping out to get my bag.

Kathleen stayed close to the cab to take it back into Dublin. She gave me another hug and wished me a safe flight. I thanked her, feeling somewhat okay, and turned to find Padraig standing behind me.

"I'll wait here," Kathleen said, as she smiled and ducked into the cab.

I just stared when Padraig reached over to take my bag, offering me his arm at the same time.

"You didn't think I'd let you leave just like that, did you?"

"But how did you get here so fast?" I'd finally found my voice. "What about work?"

"I had someone cover for me—no big deal. After you left, I couldn't do it. Hopped into a cab right behind you."

I was still thrown, but couldn't stop smiling.

"I also had to give you this." He reached into a bag I had not seen him holding and pulled out a gorgeous light green scarf. "Something else to remember me by, especially when you need a little comfort," he said, as he wrapped the thick, soft fabric around my neck. "We'll be in touch, you and I, and seeing each other before you know it. Now go and clean up the world, one word at a time."

I couldn't even laugh at him repeating my cheesy line as I tried to get a grip on my emotions. He gave me a long hug, but pulled back before I settled into him too much. Another kiss and a smile and it was time to go.

He turned towards the cab, and I turned to walk into the terminal. When I swung back for one last look, he and Kathleen were standing outside the cab, waving. I waved back, then walked through the doors.

I managed to check in quickly, despite my swirling thoughts and emotions. As I waited in the Security line, I brushed the scarf closer against my face. It smelled like him, and now the tears came in earnest. I somehow made it through the line and to the gate. People cast concerned glances my way and some may have even tried to talk to me. I just continued cuddling into my new scarf and somehow made it to my seat.

Trying to settle in, I put my earphones in to listen to music. As the engines roared for takeoff, only one thought filled my mind, repeating over and over ...

*What have I done?*

- END OF BOOK 1 -

# Kathleen and Amelia's Mix (by Amelia)

1.  The Distance – CAKE
2.  Starry, Starry Night – Josh Groban
3.  Just A Girl – No Doubt
4.  Still Haven't Found What I'm Looking For – U2
5.  Caribbean Blue – Enya
6.  Molly Malone – Gogarty's Pub Music II
7.  Dream Angus – Teresa Doyle
8.  White Shadows - Coldplay
9.  Only Time – Enya
10. Wide Open Spaces – Dixie Chicks
11. Fields of Athenry – Gogarty's Pub Music II
12. Canto Alla Vita – Josh Groban/ The Corrs
13. Summer Wine – The Corrs w/ Bono
14. I Wanna Be Bad – Willa Ford
15. Tuolumne – Eddie Vedder
16. Green Fields of France – Dropkick Murphy's
17. What If – Coldplay
18. Hilary's Theme – Dying Young Soundtrack
19. Where the Streets Have No Name – U2
20. Book of Days – Enya

# ACKNOWLEDGEMENTS

I'm so excited for the chance to re-imagine this book. What a journey—from years of writing/querying/editing, finally bringing it to light during a pandemic and shelter-in-place order, to now sharing this refreshed version. I'm so grateful for the ride.

Ireland is a special place. Each time I travel there, I find new sources of inspiration. In the scenery, the people ... I couldn't think of a better place to set my story. The characters are mainly of my imagination, but the places they visit are real and many that I've spent time in myself. A special thank you to Baggot Court Townhouse (my place in Dublin—try the Baileys oatmeal!), O'Donoghue's, The Quays (so many memories), Carrolls, Butlers chocolate shop, Bewley's café (Dublin Morning is my absolute favorite), Trinity College (I'll see the Book of Kells one of these days), Guinness Storehouse & Gravity Bar (always a must), Riversdale House B&B (I haven't fallen off the stones yet!), Waterside Guesthouse, Cullinan's Guesthouse, Lahinch Golf Club (great Irish Coffee), McGann's Pub, Gus O'Connor's Pub, and the beautiful town of Doolin—for the warm welcome and hospitality each time I've visited. I can't wait to come back soon.

While this is a work of fiction, some of the incidents are true (and I'm not telling which ones). Also, I apologize to my characters for the situations I put them in. It's purely for the good of the story, and not my own enjoyment. I'm sure they'll forgive me.

On a more serious note, I just want to say that things can get tough and not work out as we'd hoped. I think the past year has certainly shown that. Writing this novel, and the rest of the trilogy, has come from a very personal place and ultimately been a great source of healing. Whatever life throws at you, take those emotions and use them to push you forward. Don't give up—dig in. You just never know where you could end up.

Music is a very important piece of me. The right song can help heal a broken heart or struggling soul, help celebrate a triumph, maybe just give a safe backdrop for decisions you need to make or keep you company when doing chores or reading/writing. I hope you enjoyed the playlist Amelia creates for their driving time. I love making playlists myself, and have recreated this one on Spotify. You can find it (and more to come) at: http://ow.ly/XxyJ50EYoCC (sorry, I had to get creative with "Hilary's Theme"). You can also find the link on my website in the Novels section.

A big thank you to: Sarah Lee, for 20+ years of friendship and adventures (a.k.a. story ideas); Dan O'Leary, a great muse—when're we going back?; Andrea Arnold and Lisa Ramirez—here's to planning the real thing; Mark White—you're a godsend; Gladys Scott and Debra Gausebeck, for being constants through so much; Jessica Mignone, my oldest friend and NaNo buddy—your support means a lot; Carrie Sohn, for crying with me and helping with a really tough year; CP Molnar, for the best reaction; Sara Dean, Jennifer Jackson, and Meghan Bertapelle—my OGBFFs—for all the belief and support ... love you guys; Mrs. Poole, for the opportunities to write all those years ago—look what it led to; Stephanie Denton and Charlotte Tuipulotu—all those book club meetings and margaritas paid off; Jeff Deutsch, my first beta reader and a wonderful support, personally and professionally; Rhonda Abrams and Anne Marie Bonneau, for celebrating right along with me—what a year; to the staff at the Oceano, for creating such a local respite in which to write.

To Sands Press and Perry Prete—thank you for your belief in *Beginning's End* and putting it out into the world.

To Hanna, Michael, Catherine, and the publishing team at She Rises Studios—thank you for giving *Beginning's End* a new life and helping make the story even better.

To my editors Laurie and Katrina ... it's been a pleasure and the novel is better thanks to both of you.

To Auntie Kris and Uncle Jerry—thanks for being the best cheering section a girl could ask for.

To Dad—thank you for just always being there, with a listening ear or a joke … whichever I need. Another book to add to your shelf! I can't believe this day has come and am so excited to share it. Here's to those Canadian writing genes.

To Lisa, my sister and best friend—we've shared it all, from questionable bike rides as kids (handlebars!) to walks through St. Stephen's Green. You've helped me survive a hell of a year and made this all the more special—here's to the best-planned release parties. And thank you for introducing me to Ireland, one of our favorite placcs on the planet. Time to go back, for more writing material!

Finally, to my mom—who we lost recently, unexpectedly, and much too soon—I owe you everything. Thank you for the unwavering belief and space to pursue my dreams (as in my "writing desk"—really a 2nd dining room table crammed into the guest room). From late nights trying to hit a NaNoWriMo word count to standing by my side at the Cliffs of Moher as I dreamed of becoming a published author. This one's for you.

# ABOUT THE AUTHOR

*Photo Credit: Gladys White Scott*

Emily Pickard was born in Tacoma, Washington and grew up in the San Francisco Bay Area. She has been writing stories for as long as she can remember. Just ask her 5th grade teacher. Emily feels it's important to travel as much as possible and has walked the Spanish Steps, gazed out over the Cliffs of Moher, walked the lava at Kilauea, even explored Istanbul's Basilica Cistern. Ireland is one of her favorite places to visit and has been a great inspiration for her writing. When she's not reading, she can be found at a local beach.

Come visit my website! Check out my other writings and drop a note - I'd love to hear from you: www.emilypickard.com.

You can also find me on Twitter (@EmilyAPickard), Facebook (@EmilyAnnePickard), and Instagram (@eapickard).